A former U.S. Department of State Diplomatic Desk Officer for Chile, Burr Cartwright Brundage is currently professor of history at Eckerd College, St. Petersburg, Florida. He is the author of *Empire of the Incas, Lords of Cuzco,* and *A Rain of Darts: The Mexica Aztecs,* and has also published two books of poetry.

TWO EARTHS, TWO HEAVENS

TWO EARTHS, TWO HEAVENS

An Essay Contrasting the Aztecs and the Incas

Burr Cartwright Brundage

UNIVERSITY OF NEW MEXICO PRESS
Albuquerque

970.3
A9976

F
1219
.B893

dedicated to the memory
of my father
Frank Edwin Brundage

PREFACE

Any comparison of two historic enterprises—of two peoples and their pasts—can certainly sharpen the outlines of each, but it will explain neither. After the comparison has been made each will seem still to be as unique as before.

This is as it should be. In history there are no inner laws, nothing which even remotely resembles automatism, nothing which gives us the right to predict. The record of the past is a cultural "becoming" which does not lend itself to easy reductions. This insubstantiality confounds the record and in the process threatens a perpetual lapse into chaos. Yet, strangely enough, as we contemplate this welter which is the *civitas terrena*, we seem to be always just on the verge of apprehending its structure. But in the upshot we are always disappointed—we do not succeed ever in reducing the tumbling course of events to coherence.

At every step of the way an image swims before our eyes. The events themselves deny this image but we recognize it. It is of course that of the *civitas dei*, a state which never did exist on earth but one without whose corrective power and relevance history is void, banal, and sans interest. We can make judgments on no part of the past unless we have in mind the picture of the perfect state, the "divine city" wherein man was as he ought to have been. We cannot do without detailed and factual knowledge of peoples and of their record but there is also the need for this higher vision. Indeed the fact and the fiction are meaningless without each other; history is both the "was" and the "should have been." The two cannot be separated.

Comparing the tales of two nations out of the same epoch and with the same general background should enable us to experience the awe which is part of any contemplation of history, and this I suppose is the main reason for this book. To contrast two peoples as they create institutions, structures of thought, and cosmologies speaks of the incompleteness of human effort. The portrayal of the similarities between them must additionally remind us also that man and all his works are meaningful.

I have chosen here to contrapose the histories of two peoples who superficially were alike: Incas and Mexica (these latter being that one of the Aztec nations best known to us). Contrasting these two brings out their uniqueness and their creativity. Their similarities on the other hand give new meaning to their destinies. Both of these people were close to their Paleolithic backgrounds and both therefore seem almost pristine. A sense of something very human should emerge out of such a comparative enterprise and I fancy that the reader will be able to feel—beyond and outside the exotic details of their communal living—the brotherhood that binds them together.

This is an essay. It is meant not to prove any one point but to illuminate.

CONTENTS

	MEXICA	INCA*
Legendary Backgrounds	Wandering	Wandering
Beginnings	Founding of Mexico 1369	Founding of Cuzco 1250(?)
Genealogical Tradition	Acamapichtli Founds Dynasty	Manco Capac Founds Dynasty Six Rulers
Experimental Reigns	Huitzilihuitl 1391–1414 Chimalpopoca 1415–1427	Viracocha Inca 1400–1438
Crucial War in Which Empire Was Born	Tepaneca War 1427–1428	Chanca War 1438
Imperial Formulation	Itzcoatl 1427–1440 Moteuczoma I 1440–1468	Pachacuti 1438–1463 Topa Inca, Coregent 1463–1473
Imperial Plateau	Axayacatl 1469–1481 Tizoc 1481–1486 Ahuitzotl 1486–1502	Topa Inca 1473–1493 Huayna Capac (Regency) 1493–1500(?)
Period of Greatest Splendor: Hidden Weaknesses Begin To Show	Moteuczoma II 1503–1520	Huayna Capac 1500–1526
Internal Conflict and Foreign Attack	Cuitlahuac 1520 Cuauhtemoc 1520–1521	Huascar 1526–1532 Atauhuallpa 1532
Postimperial History	None	Neo-Inca State Until 1572

*The dates are in no sense as reliable as those in the Mexica column. Some of them in fact are guesswork though they are sufficient for purposes of comparison.

1

Out of the Egg

(1)

First impressions are important. As a boy I used to listen to my grandmother telling me of far-away countries. I recall that the places in South America about which she talked were the most enthralling of all. Names like those of the mountains Aconcagua and Huascarán were like echoes from a never-never land. They reverberated with hidden meanings. I do not think I ever tried to capture these meanings—I simply acknowledged them and in my imaginings settled for pictures of vast mountain walls and deserts of rock, raised to a gigantic scale. Cotopaxi meant snows floating above green valleys, quiet and full of silence. Aconcagua was a name of ineffable majesty, but the most magical of all the names was that of Titicaca, the highest lake in the world! I felt about this body of water that, for it to be on the map at all, some human eye must indeed at one moment of marvelous discovery have beheld its beauty, yet I being so small could never hope to emulate such high adventure. Only heroes could stand on its shores. Lake Titicaca was holy and serene; it lay, a plain of blue water, so high up on the world's roof that the snow-covered peaks about it were low like hills. If

someone had asked me whether I should like to visit Lake
Titicaca I would surely have declined, lost in the ambiguity that while I could not doubt its existence, neither
could I believe in it. It was enchanted.

These impressions burrowed deep and were forgotten.
Then a bit later in my boyhood career came Prescott's
Conquest of Mexico, a book which opened up a world this
time not of mystery but of deeds. The names in this
Mexican world stamped themselves differently on my
mind than those from South America. Orizaba, the
sentinel mountain, reared itself up on a picture postcard
horizon; it was done in blues and green and gold, almost
medieval. Then followed the witchery of such names as
Popocatepetl and Iztaccihuatl. Impossible names! Combi-
nations of vowels and consonants done in this manner
drew my eye and I longed to hear them spoken. Also
another lake appeared but one real enough to have
attracted real events, events such as the meeting of Cortés
and Moteuczoma, the terror and suspense of the *noche
triste,* and the capture of Cuauhtemoc. Lake Tezcoco
(Texcoco), in which stood the Aztec city of Mexico, I
could believe in and even hope some day to see.

Maturity brought on a kind of a somnolence in the
midst of so much meaning. Now, after years of research,
writing, and many visits to these places, I am occasionally
aware of them with the vividness of my first impressions.
Mexico is for me a stage upon which violence and
splendid achievements are at home; the landscape reveals
the quality of its history. Peru on the contrary is a
presence. And even the events brought to pass in that land
by Incas and Spaniards pale into insignificance beside the
fact of Peru itself. I can believe that I have been to Mexico.
I cannot believe that I have ever been to Peru. I am sure
that for me the history of the Aztecs takes its hues from

Prescott, lurid and enamelled. The history of the Incas seems on the contrary alien and monolithic, grey and monstrously rational—truly a record from another world. What I am hereby submitting to the reader is therefore a palimpsest of impressions. It is the result of painstaking research written over a boy's sense of wonder, and I do not know which is more important.

(2)

I shall begin by considering whom these folk *claimed* to be as opposed to whom they really *were*. At this level we find that they share a basic kinship. Inca and Aztec myths of origins in fact could almost be interchanged. This in spite of the vast extent of jungles, mountains, and coastal waters separating them and precluding the possibility of either one of them directly borrowing from the other.

Both peoples believed they were cave-born. The Aztecs came from Chicomoztoc ("Seven Caves") while the Incas emerged from four caves in Pacaritambo ("Origin Lodge"). It is interesting that the Incas had a specific location for Pacaritambo and installed a cult there, whereas the Aztecs could only point vaguely to the northwest as the direction in which one would have to travel to finally reach their place of origin. Efforts which later Aztec rulers made to discover the lost Chicomoztoc were fruitless. The Incas handled history more simply and probably more competently for they arbitrarily identified a site as Pacaritambo and thenceforth brooked no doubting.

The Inca epic begins with a heroic founder named Manco Capac, his three brothers and the four wives. Each of the four couples emerged from clefts in the cathedral-like rock of Pacaritambo, each cleft named after a different tribal affiliation. In the myth the sun-god had designated Manco Capac as his son and had commissioned him to lead this group on a pilgrimage which would end when they had founded a city destined to become the seat of a world empire.

This mission Manco performed with piety and courage. En route the brothers fell away, being either apotheosized or otherwise disappearing from the story, and this left the line of Manco to dominate the end of the tale, which was the founding of the holy city of Cuzco and the whole subsequent history of the Incas. Manco himself was of the Tampu *ayllu* or lineage, and the leadership he exercised was simply legend's way of stating that, of the four ayllus that combined to become the Incas, the Tampu family was that one which claimed the commanding position—and ultimately of course the imperial office.

Manco was undoubtedly a real personage, but his three brothers are merely thinly disguised versions of the *huacas* or demi-gods worshipped by the other three tribes. The *huaca* revered by Manco's group was known as Inti and he is accordingly presented to us as being on a higher level of godhead than any of the three brothers. Inti would soon be confused with the sun and, in the later career of the Incas, was to become identical with him.

The four wives, including Mama Ocllo—Manco Capac's wife, turn out to be—as one would expect—those earth or corn goddesses brought in by each of the four groups. In the original charge made by the sun to Manco, he had prophesied that the site of Cuzco was to be on that exact spot where Mama Ocllo's golden digging-stick would sink into the ground of its own volition.

There were the expected trials along the route of the wandering. As we might expect from our sources, the name of each settling is meticulously recorded along with the number of years of their residence in each place. Wherever needed, Inti gave oracles which guided the footsteps of these homeless ones and saved them from great perils. In the Huatanay Valley the Incas came at last to the end of their hegira. Here they allied with certain indigenous groups, defeated and scattered others and finally, as the fulfillment of the prophecy, settled on the site of Cuzco.

There remained only the second part of their commission, the injunction that they should wax powerful and, using Cuzco as a center, should reach out to possess the four quarters of the world.

We turn now to the Aztecs. They believed themselves to have been a grouping of seven peoples. The sacred caves out of which they emerged were located on a mythical island called Aztlan in the middle of a lake. Each of the tribes left Aztlan at the instigation of oracles from their respective gods, though the command to them to conquer the world is not as unequivocally given as in the Inca legend. Nor are the leaders of the various groups named with the same precision, for the god was more important among the Aztecs than the leader who did his bidding. All in all, however, this tale of wandering is remarkably like the Inca story. Places through which the Aztecs passed are also carefully remembered, along with specific dates.

At one point we do find something significantly different in the story of the Aztec exodus and that is the incident of how the tribe of the Mexica came to be separated and somewhat distinct from their kindred. Miraculously, a tree under which the seven tribes were feasting broke in two and the god Huitzilopochtli spoke out of it designating the Mexica as his chosen people and prophesying for them a splendid destiny. The other tribes thereupon went off in other directions leaving the Mexica to their own devices. It is only at this point in the tale that the Mexica begin to play the part of the Tampu in the Inca story. No one ancestor or leader, however, is singled out in the Mexican account as a precursor specially to be revered. This is a notable divergence.

The Mexica lagged far behind the other more active Aztec groups, but this gave them the opportunity to learn that war was not only a desirable but also a sacred human activity. It was the god who instructed them. Huitzilo-pochtli appears in the tale as a surrogate for the sun, one who is conceived to be a heavenly warrior nourished by blood shed on the battlefield. Goddesses also appear in the story, generally alien and hostile.

As they passed through the ruins of Tula, formerly the seat of a vast empire and the reputed home of all historic virtues, some of its grandeur rubbed off on the Mexica and they acquired thereby a peculiar destiny. This contact of the Mexica with the ruins of an empire from the past takes the place in the Inca myth of the sun's adjuration to Manco to rule the world.

The Mexica finally entered the great basin in which was situated Lake Tezcoco. Here, after enduring much, they founded their city of destiny, the spot being made known to them by a sign from the god. Out in the shoals of the lake an eagle was seen seated on a cactus tree and bearing in his beak the flowing hieroglyph which meant war (later this scroll was interpreted to be a serpent). The Mexica had been attracted to this arcane spot when the heart of a sacrificed captive had been hurled blindly out into the reed thickets.

Every time I consider such presumptuous legends as these—tales told to authenticate the conquering role of a people in history—I am impressed by their naïve directness. They were supposed to be believed without reservation even though the authenticating gods in each case were only the local fetishes of originally insignificant tribes and were in no sense mighty lords of creation lending universality to the tales. People who imagined their past in such a way were certainly no Byzantine sophisticates with centuries of history behind them. They were earnest folk but untried. In the Mount Sinai story the quality of history is known to be contractual and therefore contingent. In the two tales of wandering we are considering here, however, we are in the childhood of the world and we perceive no such subleties.

(3)

Behind these legends lie the real histories.

Both the Incas and Aztecs were fairly nondescript peoples, possibly polyglot and certainly in the beginning bound together in their respective communities more by hope and common poverty than by ties of blood. Both were noted for their toughness and both acquired unenviable reputations for arrogance. The Aztecs were particularly noted for their ferocity in war, the Incas for their guile. Both were thoroughly hated by the peoples among whom their lines were to be cast.

It is difficult to evaluate the effects which the contrasting terrains may have had upon the two peoples. The Incas were a people of the Andes, born and bred to a life lived at altitudes averaging eleven thousand feet. We would normally guess that the Andes and the greatly broken country of the Peruvian *altiplano* would impose isolation and passivity upon resident peoples along with a total concentration upon the wresting of a livelihood from the soil. Such was not the case. The world of the Andes was a highway for many groups; movement was constant and normal. Thus a world which we today judge to be harsh and forbidding did not repress civilization as straitly as we imagine.

I suspect that what the grandeur and difficulty of the Peruvian terrain did to the ethos of the Incas was to set them against separatism and diversity simply because that was the way they were supposed to go. In a very short time they were to achieve a sense of policy and a concept of administrative proficiency—all things which are necessary to the rise of an axial state. To my way of thinking, the broken world of the Andes acted on the Incas as an "in-spite-of." They were contemptuous of the shackles laid on them by the land itself; they managed almost with ease to circumvent its asperities. However, we must in fairness note that their policy had no ulterior vision in it—as we will see, it was narrow, self-indulgent, and entertained no doubts. Its narrowness repeats the narrowness of the Andean valleys; its sublimity imitated the surrounding Andean peaks.

The Aztecs—among whom the Mexica were only one tribe—were a people very aware of their Chichimec or barbarian descent, and this fact sometimes had a damping effect on the efforts which they made to appear outsize. The Chichimecs inhabited the relatively open steppe country which stretched away to the north and west of that great basin in which the Mexica were to finally settle. The average elevation of this steppe was no more than seven thousand feet.

The Chichimecs were mainly hunters and gatherers. Those groups influenced by residence near the few merchant outposts established among them grew their own food. They were a dispersed people and therefore quite wild. Accurate bowmen, they early adapted to a life of war when in contact with imperial cultures. The expanses of the Mesoamerican plateau and its excellent vistas seemed to draw these people away from things but never toward anything. Their horizons were not closely hemmed in with towering mountains, each snowcapped and ringed with thunders, such as in Peru blocked a limitless vision. Whereas the Andes formed no impenetrable barrier to the Peruvian traveller in spite of their gigantic ranges and awesome canyons, the Mesoamerican world positively invited movement and interchange. Peru was never the land of merchants, fairs, and far-wanderers that Mesoamerica was and had been from its earliest days.

In their political culture we shall discover that all the Aztec groups were exceptionally volatile; we can certainly derive this in part from the openness of their geography. Echoing the catholicity of their physical surroundings, the conceptual world of the Aztecs was pluralistic and their polities correspondingly weak. No Aztec state ever achieved the concept of total centrality as did Cuzco. The Aztec city-states were to spring up in a land various in its ways of life, a great arena where polities clashed constantly against each other.

(4)

I do not believe that anybody really knows how the Incas and Aztecs were socially arranged as they moved from their reputed places of origin to the founding of their cities. Those Chichimecs who were to become Aztecs quite early mingled with broken bits of urban-oriented folk, which fact makes any guesswork in regard to them difficult. As for the Incas we know that they were organized into ayllus, a very old Peruvian type of community and one with a strong sense of territory. The Incas appear to have partially forsaken this type of society as they moved about in the seminomadic and outlaw phase of their early existence. Once they had founded Cuzco, however, and staked out their claims to the fields round about, they seem to have reverted to full ayllu organization.

Among the Aztecs the name of the corresponding field-oriented community was the *calpulli.* The ayllu and the calpulli appear to have been quite similar. Both owned lands communally and periodically redistributed the fields according to fluctuations in the size of the component families. The calpulli found its center geographically around a shrine or temple erected on a pyramid base; the ayllu on the contrary was focused in a stone fetish or a skull representing the "grandfather" or old ancestor. Both organizations were regulated by headmen or elders but could elect specially able warriors to lead them in time of war. The ayllu appears to have had a pronounced familial tinge. The calpulli could easily be translated into a ward or section of a city. The ayllu in distinction appears to have been more tenacious of its traditions.

Both Mexican and Inca peoples were conglomerates of calpullis and ayllus, respectively, and when later they had founded their cities they conceived of the latter not only as conferring a common citizenship but as guaranteeing several lesser citizenships as well.

I think this heterogeneous character of our two peoples had much to do with their later social structures, particularly in the prominence of lineage nobilities in both.

(5)

As acorns are to mighty oaks so were the mascot gods of these early wanderers to the later imperial deities who were to arise and sanction great conquests. Inti and Huitzilopochtli had this in common, that they both had histories. I see the spasmodic transformations of these two fetishes into higher deities reflecting accurately the rise of the two tribes to greatness.

Inti was originally the talisman of the original men of Manco and was carried about in a small wicker container. The fetish itself appears to have been a dried bird, most likely a hawk, and this object, when properly petitioned, gave oracles and leadership to the tribe. It was he, the luck and destiny of the people, who led them to the site of Cuzco.

As the Incas extended their power, Inti came increasingly under the domination of the ruling house; his shrine was soon by fiat the focal point of all Cuzco. While this was happening, however, his obviously parochial and demonic origins had to be expunged and a higher status created for him. This was achieved by identifying him with the lordly sun which held imperial sway over the heavens. Thus Inti was a conflation of two opposing concepts of divinity; he remained as the soul or luck of a discrete people, but he added to it a solar statement of their superiority over all other peoples. Inti's image in Cuzco ceased to be exclusively a tattered and mummified bird but became additionally a round gold plate representing the sun disk and set in the walls of his temple where the rays of the sun at dawn would set it flashing and reverberating.

Huitzilopochtli was originally named Mexi, from which his people, the Mexica, took their name. It is quite

possible that the name Huitzilopochtli was the name of
one of his early charismatic sorcerers or oracle-priests and
that, at the death of said person, the deity and the man
were fused. However that may be, his nature is clear—he
was the destiny of the tribe and also the one who sent the
people forth and guided them with oracles. In representa-
tions he is shown carried in a god-bundle on the back of a
special priest. Here he is depicted as a hummingbird.

Huitzilopochtli's special forte—outside of his mascot's
role—was war, for he taught the Mexica while on their
historic trek how to sacrifice those taken on the field of
battle. And later, as we might expect, once the Mexica had
attained stature in the broad, new Aztec world, Huitzilopochtli was further identified with the sun.

These mascot gods who accompanied their peoples
were in no sense unique—many such ragamuffin tribes in
history had talismanic deities who represented them and
indeed who *were* their very essences. Where these two
deities differed from the run-of-the-mill mascot gods lies
in the fact that the two people whom they guided attained
to greatness. This forced the respective deities to rapidly
accommodate themselves; they had to reflect each new
militant and imperialistic stance which the state adopted.
This is why, without at the same time losing their close
identity with the tribe, they could each become the sun. I
shall comment later on the specific problems that were to
arise from this apotheosis, that is, their rise from the
talismanic level to the status of kingly gods.

(6)

The business of the upgrading of a people's god as a
response to geographic expansion is a mechanic in history

whose complexity has not often been probed. Here I would like to explore this as background to later statements which will be made about Inti and Huitzilopochtli.

An individual has no need ever to alter the face of the god whom he worships. His only choice comes in asking himself whether or not he wishes to gaze directly into that divine face. The individual looks at his creator as beyond his comprehension yet always as the master of rightness, ineffable but still present in the way a person is present. However, when individuals coalesce into a state—which is what we are discussing here—the god is treated differently. They manipulate the god so that to them and to others he will appear as a surety for the state—its founder, protector, and constant supporter. The corollary of this is that the state announces itself to be a surrogate of the god or, as in our day, of God Himself. God's rescripts can then be found in the policies and official utterances of the state.

But always at this point a terrible and most pathetic confusion arises in the state. The state has become what it is by having evolved through a series of historical experiences. Lineages became clans, which in turn became tribes, then chiefdoms, then states—each having produced its own societal view of the divine. But at each of these levels the vision perforce differs, and taken together they are all of them generically unlike the individual's vision of god.

They are not only unlike each other but generally incompatible as well. The spirit that is Inti, leader and luck of a wandering group, has not the prestige of the god needed by a growing and ambitious people clustered in a central city and already beginning to reach out expectantly to the larger world around them. Yet when Inti assumes, as his highest and greatest avatar, the sun's attributes, he cannot thereby cancel his more primitive self. This is merely another way of saying that an evolving state cannot fully erase its past and achieve a pure policy; its component parts, its more ancient selves continue and only great strife or long years will subdue or alter them.

The god of a community is not a symbol of God at all. He is rather a symbol of the community in its highest aspirations. Thus he must change in proportion as the community grows or dwindles, whereas *my* god or *yours* cannot and does not change, for our unprotected lives can no more rise to challenge or to warp ultimacy than can the summer breeze topple a mountain.

The state, by the trick of setting itself up as an effective arbiter of society, persuades itself that it can not only influence ultimacy but also that it stands in for it in all instances. Where the state is finally confounded is in the built-in lack of compatibility between the several faces of God representing the various periods in the city's growth. Thus, though it claims to speak with a single voice, the state never really does; it is too many things within itself. The state staggers and because of this it cannot successfully legislate the dogma that it is truly God's surrogate.

Huitzilopochtli is an excellent case in point. As a giver of oracles to his people when they were emigrating from Aztlan, he stood for the survival of the group. He was an earnest that the group would find food and shelter, that its offspring would survive, and that its ambushes would succeed where those of others failed. In such a world Huitzilopochtli lived in vivid and democratic conflict with other gods of equal or greater powers.

When the Mexica settled on the two islands which together made up the city of Mexico in Lake Tezcoco and began to follow a script of continuous warfare, they were under the domination of the Tepaneca people; they had moved from the concrete world of survival into something more abstract—for their life of war was now becoming something of an end in itself and needed to be validated. Consequently, Huitzilopochtli added to his roles that of a patron of war. But survival and the seeking of war do not always match and Huitzilopochtli's two natures from that point on did not therefore necessarily correspond. When on top of this Huitzilopochtli was called upon to be master of the empire that later sprang up under the aegis of Mexico, he should also have assumed another avatar, that of a universal god. He failed to do this. This contradiction and weakness in the Mexican's vision of God, as we shall see later, came from his inability to conceive of a total sovereignty on earth.

Inti's early progress was much the same. He added to his role as the luck of the Incas the role of the conquering sun, which was further defined as the lord of the Inca state. The difference between the two gods lies in the fact that full empire did come to the Incas; accordingly and necessarily they therefore saw their god now as a universal sustainer. But they turned aside from casting Inti in this higher role and raised up instead a more suitable god, Viracocha, who was not simply a higher personation of Inti but an autonomous god in his own right. Inti was thereby demeaned but he could not be erased—his mere presence continued to somewhat addle the purposes of the state and when the end came and the empire collapsed, the Incas were first to jettison Viracocha, then Inti, and finally even the most primitive of their early gods.

Being built up of incongruous historical tiers, the state cannot create for itself a god unaffected by those incongruities. To obtain a clear view of a state which has become an empire, one must begin by observing the composite god whom it has finally evoked.

(7)

When the Incas in their wandering moved into the narrow Huatanay Valley, pushing finally into its upper part which commanded the great north-south Andean passageway, they were blocked from going any further. Here they settled and survived by a mixture of accommodation, insolence, and cunning. They insinuated themselves into the neighboring communities, made alliances, truckled when they had to, seized lands whenever the chance presented itself, and made arrangements with folk more numerous than they were. And they grew.

I do not know what we should really call this kind of toughness. It appears occasionally in history and always turns out on hindsight to be the cornerstone of a people's later greatness. If we class it as blind indomitability we are wrong, for it is allied with astuteness in the beginning. It is calculation and pliancy together, allied to a contempt for suffering, whether the suffering of others or of oneself. It is dictated by an overpowering desire to survive, but there also has to be present a sense of destiny—a feeling, however vague, for greatness, an appreciation, however dim, that the future can be different from and mightier than the past, in short an ability to deal in policy as against routine requirements for survival.

The Incas had this to perfection. Once they had dispersed a weaker people called the Huallas who lived on the interfluvial ridge of Cuzco and took over their agricultural terraces, their arrogance made them from that point on a major irritant in the small world of the valley. They were thoroughly disliked; indeed, for their repeated treacheries, they were consummately hated. Whereas each of the Peruvian hamlets around them were locked into the harsh business of raising crops at high altitudes and therefore were unable to conceive of anything much beyond that, the Incas found time to scheme and plot and manipulate the more naïve peoples around them. This orientation toward a future is what distinguished them from their neighbors.

Once the Mexica had entered the basin in which Lake Tezcoco was situated, they similarly made their mark. They settled in Chapultepec, a rock jutting out into the lake, and for a whole generation they built up the reputation of being dangerous and even more than normally ruthless. Then followed their terrible defeat at the hands of justly incensed neighbors, their dispersal, and virtual enslavement. But even reduced as they were to menial tasks, their actions and attitudes continued to be such that the suspicions and distrust of their masters and neighbors were never allayed. They were in fact a people known to prepare all kinds of evils for others. Instead of guile, the hallmark of the Incas, the Mexica Aztecs specialized in ferocity. The whole Aztec world which was then aborning was noted for its dedication to war, but none carried this characteristic further than the Mexica. Whereas the Incas were clever, the Mexica were intransigent. Both were aware of ends but whereas the Mexica project for greatness was dictated by religious mania, the corresponding Inca drive was a concern to dominate others.

(8)

One of the most curious similarities between the two peoples is found in their almost exact contemporaneity.

The part of the pre-Columbian world we are dealing with is distinguished by anthropologists as Nuclear America. Geographically this area runs from central Mexico through Central America and into the Andean area of South America as far down as what is today northern Bolivia. Thus the area includes all of the high cultures of pre-Columbian America including the Aztec and Inca. Archaeology has confirmed the thesis that gave rise to this terminology, namely that such regions as Peru and Mexico, though greatly separated, developed together and in concert. Mesoamerica and Peru passed back and forth such things as maize, cult attitudes, and metallurgy; they moved through essentially the same stages of culture and at approximately the same times, even though each area was unaware of the other's existence.

Artifactual evidence thus allows us to predicate broadly similar backgrounds for both Inca and Aztec. But this establishes only a family, not necessarily a fraternal, resemblance. Historical as opposed to archaeological research is a luxury field in Nuclear America for it can only operate where textual evidence is available, and this means that only the Inca and Aztec experience can be clearly known—with Toltec, Maya, and Chimú dimly glimpsed at best. This means that only in the case of Inca and Aztec can we investigate the discontinuities as well as the likenesses in their histories.

The underlying similarities in chronology must first be noted. Previous civilizations had existed in the areas that the Incas and Aztecs occupied. In the case of the Incas the predecessor horizon culture had two important centers, one at Tiahuanacu and one at Huari, both of which appear to have been imperial centers. These empires seem to have ended about A.D. 800. This can be matched by the fall of the empire of Teotihuacán in Mesoamerica perhaps about A.D. 750. The fall of these two imperial civilizations profoundly unsettled our two widely separated parts of

Nuclear America. The final cultural reformulations which appeared were the two in which we are presently interested.

But there is a significant difference. Following the fall of the Peruvian empires in the ninth century, city life stagnated in Peru until the rise of Cuzco and other contemporary states centuries later. There was in other words something of a cultural depression preceding the Inca empire which gave to Cuzco a past without a model upon which she might easily pattern herself. In Mesoamerica things did not move that way, for city life continued after the fall of Teotihuacán and produced the vigorous Toltec empire which did not itself fall traditionally until A.D. 1168. The Aztec states—and Mexico in particular—thus had a near and prestigious exemplar to copy as they could. The movement of displaced persons made known to us in the wandering tales of the Incas and Aztecs may have begun more or less contemporaneously, but only the latter were close enough to the influence of a prototype to be affected. We shall see shortly what eventuated from this difference.

Our two peoples had ended their respective peregrinations by settling in new homes; Cuzco was founded at some time in the last half of the thirteenth century and Mexico traditionally in 1369. The near coincidence in time here is again striking and makes us realize that we are dealing with members of an authentic genus of nations.

2

First Cities

(1)

Some of my friends have laughed at my penchant for ruins. Whereas the average tourist visits a country to see "the sights" which primarily include street scenes, restaurants, inhabited buildings, and amusements, I generally go first to see a country's ruins. Yet I willingly grant that toppled blocks and excavated stumps of walls have meaning only when the modern descendants of those who constructed the antiquities live among the mute stones, house themselves in them, make love there, defy others across their walls, and engrave upon them their own green epitaphs. A ruin holds for me virtue only as it is embedded in the whole context of time. A ruin on the moon would certainly be astounding but it would have no meaning. I think it best here to define what I mean by a ruin.

A ruin in fact is a very present voice, but not sharp and preemptory. Its voice is deceptively ventriloquial; it seems to issue from the mouths of the dead but it speaks of things breathing and very near, very much a part of our own living. Voices from ruins take on a sardonic quality;

they whisper about the silliness of striving and then immediately remind us that we too strive lest we cease to be—a paradox. Voices from ruins are thus not empty answers like echoes from bare rock walls, but are questions, continually repeated and flung back at us. Ruins are never the records of total strangers.

My first view of Cuzco was from the air as our rickety and unpressurized plane burst out from a pass in the Andes and rounded down on the city. The dull red tiles of the roofs, the hollow squares of the city blocks, spoke clearly of its colonial past. Then followed walks through the cold streets, greeted by fantastic Inca masonry at every turn, around every corner! Here history lived in a kind of subpresent. It seemed that at any instant the Inca past could suck the precarious present back into it, absorbing it completely. You had only to press your palm against the surface of any wall to feel the reverberations of Incas shouting, of the sharp commands that built the city of Pachacuti, the great emperor, and of the hollow murmur of conch shell trumpets celebrating the return of the first armies. Even the trucks rolling by, the ragged bootblacks importuning the tourist, and the stout matrons selling lottery tickets did not dampen these vibrations.

On the mountains, overlooking the city, is sited the most awesome ruin in South America, the showplace of Inca pride and its fortress, Sacsahuaman. I think now of Sacsahuaman, under whose walls Juan Pizarro received his death wound, as I might recall the bleached and ribbed skeleton of a mastodon. Here was not merely the simulacrum of a former existence, but the menace of true being. On those quiet battlements looking down on the roofs of the city and far out toward Mount Ausangate, I construed with Caesar, great man of action, the paradox of acting historically. In Shakespeare's words:

This common body
Like a vagabond flag upon the stream,
Goes to and back, lackeying the varying tide,
To rot itself with motion.

At the busy downtown corner of Guatemala and
Argentina in Mexico City, today's traffic rumbles over an
excavation which extends well in under the street. In this
drab and austere hole, into which absentmindedly peer
those people waiting to catch their trolleys or buses, a
stone serpent's head stretches out along a plinth some ten
or twelve feet below the present surface. This was ground
level in 1519 and the serpent's head lay at the bottom of a
balustrade that reached up to the top of the great pyramid,
the home of Huitzilopochtli. "Then" and "now" are
clearly represented here as in Cuzco, but there is a
difference.

Here in Mexico the stones sleep. They are curios,
survivals and artifacts out of the past. They are the ejecta
from a completed era—like the fallen bust of Ozymandias.
They affect us with a noble nostalgia but they do not
threaten us as do the faceless stones of Cuzco. I do not
know why this should be so.

Only when men have gathered in cities have they
spoken with full historical authority—and their stones
after them. Cities are the greatest of human artifacts.

(2)

We may as well accept our two peoples at their word
and grant that the founding of the cities they were later to
convert into imperial capitals were the events which
defined them basically as nations. When they came to

elaborate their legends in the later period, they insisted that these settlements were made in response to signs. In other words, they expected the world to judge their historical virtue in accordance with the care they took to position themselves correctly in the first instance. "Correctly" meant in accordance with the divine will.

What has always struck me first about these famous cities is the fact that they were divided into two contrasting parts, "moieties" as they are called in the learned literature. In the case of the Inca foundation the two parts were known as Upper and Lower Cuzco respectively, a line of physical separation cutting across the sacred triangle between the Huatanay and the Tullu rivers and dividing the ridge into two parts. Upper Cuzco was preponderantly the section inhabited by the emperors and the more recent ayllus; Lower Cuzco was in the narrower apex of the triangle and served as the residence of the less successful but certainly no less numerous Inca ayllus.

Mexico—a Venice-like city built on slime and log foundations in a lake—was also divided into two moieties of the Mexica. One group, the Tenochca, inhabited the larger shoal which was called appropriately Tenochtitlan. Just to the north of it and separated only by several yards of water was the island called Tlatilulco—here had settled the other half of the tribe whom we know as the Tlatilulca.

Moieties are instituted by tribes and chiefdoms in order to standardize (and therefore to make subject to authority) the divisive tendencies present in all human communities. Thus both Cuzco and Mexico were acknowledged to be of one blood and yet were each internally competitive. When the Inca army marched, it always marched in two regiments, Upper and Lower Cuzco respectively, each commanded by a general of its own membership. At one point, in the reign of Huayna Capac, the bitterness that characterized these fraternal bodies broke out into open mutiny and was ultimately resolved only by an imposed accommodation. Division between the two parts of the Mexica broke out into actual warfare in the reign of Axayacatl (1473); this eventuated in the crushing of Tlatilulco and the imposition upon it by the Tenochca of military government.

This twofold division of the cities—this special device to achieve order—ended by splitting them asunder in their last days. The war between Huascar and Atauhuallpa, which so weakened the state at the moment of the Spaniards' arrival, can with some precision be attributed to this rivalry. Huascar, who belonged to Upper Cuzco, had in anger removed himself from its rolls because he believed that it supported his hated brother Atauhuallpa. Similarly, as the Spaniards were about to mount their last massive attack upon Mexico, the moiety of the Tenochca was ousted from its traditional leadership of the state, probably because of the previous excesses of Moteuczoma II, himself a Tenochca. Many of the leaders of that group were proscribed and done away with, which so weakened Tenochtitlan that when the attack came it straightaway collapsed, leaving the defense of the whole city to the Tlatilulca.

Thus the dual system characterizing the constitutions of both cities turned out in the end to be a sensational weakness leading directly to the overthrow of the two states by the Spaniards. While the principle was in operation, however, during the *floruit* of each people, it was used by each in a distinctive manner.

In the Mexican case there were two cities which, although side by side in the waters of the lake, had been founded at slightly different times. Each of the cities had a different orientation. Tlatilulco was Mexican with a heavy overlay of Tepaneca nobility, the Tepaneca being an important Aztec people on the western shore of the lake. Indeed the ruling house of Tlatilulco was wholly Tepaneca. Tenochtitlan on the other hand was connected through its nobility with the Culua people on the south side of the lake. The two halves of the Mexica were thus rather acutely differentiated, not only in the fact that since the disaster at Chapultepec they had had different histories, but also that they lived in what amounted to separate cities. After 1473 Tlatilulco was a defeated city; the Tlatilulca became essentially a tribute-paying people living in a sizable ward attached to Tenochtitlan, their ruling house deposed.

Only after 1473 therefore was it possible for the Mexica to act in total unison under one polity, in this case, Tenochca. This subjugation of Tlatilulco to the Tenochca wing of the Mexican people may have closed by *force majeur* the constitutionally approved division between them, but it offered no new principle of unity in its place —a spiritual division remained and resentment continued. Mexico was thus prevented from taking full advantage of its solution to the problem of disunity via moieties.

In the Inca case Cuzco was one city divided geographically by a line separating the upper from the lower moiety. The overpowering concept of autocratic rule established by Pachacuti, the greatest of the emperors, maintained the Inca emphasis on cooperation for a common end. While Lower Cuzco always had its own warchief, as we have noted, there was only one emperor and therefore only one policy. The moiety system among the Incas therefore did not impede the administration of the state. The political system which Pachacuti instituted was a unitary imperial rule; it was successfully imposed and so the earlier constitution of the state, sanctifying as it did a twofold division, was forced back into the shadows. It was Huascar's ineptitude at the very end which allowed the traditional cleavage finally to wreck the state.

(3)

As against this constitutional division of the society into two parts, which was characteristic of both Incas and Mexica, there was another traditional division principle which marked them—this was a division into four parts.

Four was the sacred number in both societies, superlatively so among the Aztecs. The common name for the Inca empire was Tahuantinsuyo which is translated as The Four Quarters. Cuzco was conceived to lie at the joining point of all four. Out from the central plaza of the city ran four trunk roads, each leading to the farthest confines of the respective quarters which they served. Administratively each quarter was ruled by a vicegerent resident in Cuzco and these four constituted an inner council of state advising the emperor.

Aztec cosmology—going far back into pre-Aztec times—conceived of the world as subject to a quadruple topographical distinction. Each of the four directions was under a unique destiny and a special color was used to symbolize it. This concept so ruled Aztec thinking that it was carried down into the structure of the state. Where at all possible an Aztec nation was composed of or artificially divided into four geographic sectors or tribal allocations, conforming thus to the structure of the world. The city of Tenochtitlan was split into four named quarters and a council of four princes formed the highest consultative and electoral body in the state. The main temple area was placed centrally at the juncture of the four quarters.

Thus each of our cities represented the radial point in a universal whole which was divided into the four parts of the compass. Each city in its own way mirrored the cosmos. Cuzco indeed was thought to be the most holy single huaca in the world because of this centrality; no ruler was legitimate who was not crowned within the city.

Of the two, Cuzco was the city most consciously embedded in the divine, the one which most graphically displayed its sacramental characteristics. This was done through the *ceque* system, surely one of man's most original urban fabrications.

Starting from the assumption that the city was the focal point of the universe, lines of spiritual force were supposed to emanate outward from it (specifically from Coricancha, the nuclear temple) like the lines that mark a magnetic field. Along each line—of which there were forty-one in all—certain huacas, or holy places, were designated. The various ayllus comprising the Inca people were each allotted one or more of these radiating lines and owed cult service to each huaca thereon. The distance one could travel outward in a half a day generally marked the site of the last huaca, whether it was a spring, a tree, a rock, a tomb, or some other object or edifice. Coricancha, the central temple which represented the dynamic heart of the system, was reserved for cult purposes to the family of the ruling emperor. Finally all of the lines were grouped into four quarters or arcs of the world circle, as we might well guess.

There was nothing as imaginatively conceived as that in Mexico, and we must therefore grant to the Incas a superior ceremonial skill. The Mexica saw their city as being under the protection of Huitzilopochtli and as the home of many powerful Mesoamerican gods; but the position of Mexico—set apart as it was in the midst of a lake—prevented its ties to the divine from being made visual and immediate. The Mexica felt their focal city to be just as closely enmeshed in the web of the gods as did the Incas, but they failed to express it practically with the same concreteness and singleness. Their connection with the divine was expressed in particularly vivid terms in the activities of war and sacrifice as well as in a multiplicity of cults. The Mexica were not organizers.

This now leads us to the discovery of another profound distinction between the two cities: Cuzco was not in any real sense a city at all, if by city we mean an area where a large number of people are concentrated as permanent residents and where they carry on diverse and often disconnected occupations. Mexico on the contrary was a true city, cosmopolitan and occupationally varied; it possessed wards where the canoeists lived and worked, where merchants, featherworkers, gardeners, priests, and foreign nobles of many social levels had their habitations. Within the city, trade was actively carried on in the famous Tlatilulco market. The many tiny mud platforms and shoals out from the edges of the city, bearing houses or gardens, were of course all part of the central city and its activities.

Cuzco on the contrary was sharply and narrowly defined by the two streams forming its two sides and by the fortified height of Sacsahuaman which closed the base of the triangle. Within this area only the residences of the inner Inca families were allowed. The life lived by this chosen few and by their servitors was purely ceremonial and administrative. Commoners did not live there and all affairs concerned with the market place were relegated to the outside. Commoners without a valid reason for being there were strictly excluded from the city. Cuzco was a city of nobles. The only events which ever stirred it were the stately festivals marking the year's progress, the reception of embassies, and the care and honoring of living and dead emperors and of the gods secluded in Coricancha. The prosaic tasks that are necessary to the life of an important city were all carried on in the many hamlets and suburbs lying out in the valley.

Cuzco in brief was a sacred and elitist site—not a true city in the sense in which Mexico was. The meaning of this becomes apparent when we realize that there was basically only one Inca city (Cuzco) whereas there were numerous Aztec cities, Mexico being only one of them.

I am sure that a closer analysis of the conceptual backgrounds of these two cities would lead one deeper into the whole meaning of their two peoples, their aspirations, and, particularly, the limits they set on their roles in history. I have space here only for a cursory glance.

(4)

The two cities had contrasting methods of adding population. Being composed exclusively of the households of the incumbent emperor and his imperial ancestors, Cuzco could only grow at the death of an incumbent; in other words, when the successor emperor began to build his royal residence within the sacred triangle and organize his own household within it. Cuzco was like a museum housing a set of pieces from the past. One piece, however, was always the cynosure of all eyes, the most glittering of them all; this was the ruling emperor. He trained this centrality and splendor until it came his time to be retired to the permanent collection as his heir was enthroned. This was growth by succession but it lacked the quality of change.

Awash in the waters of its lake, Mexico had no perceptible limits and could therefore grow as need dictated, additional *chinampas* (truck gardens) being constantly formed on its peripheries and later serving as terraces for villas or other buildings as the central city expanded. Mexico grew by accretion. Refugees, buccellarian bands, new allies, or colonies of artisans would be brought in either when needed, or on their own petition, and enrolled in the city. It was a dynamic growth, relatively uncontrolled and constantly imposing new strains on the body politic. The city therefore did not possess the same sacredness as did Cuzco which perforce remained intact and homogeneous.

This was not to say that Mexico was disorganized. The calpullis comprising the early Mexica had settled around the area of Huitzilopochtli's shrine at the meeting point of the already described four quarters. As new calpullis were formed around these or as they petitioned for admission from the outside, they were each named, organized about a local shrine, and formally placed under the jurisdiction of the appropriate quarter. Thus the city expanded rationally.

Much can be learned about the two peoples from this difference in the way they grew. What strikes us first is the fact that for the Incas time could have no surprises; it could only endlessly repeat itself—in the expansion processes of the holy city, the set and sovereign forms of the past. Time was abeyant. It existed—as witness the passage from one emperor to the next—but it did not move. The Inca caste was monolithic and of one substance; radical change could not be expected in it. There

could be no cavilling against the claim that the prerogatives of the Incas were divinely given; they therefore could
not change like other men and their right to rule was
irrefutable.

How differently the city of Mexico bespoke the peoples
who inhabited it! Some were base commoners, some
nobles, some slaves, some peripatetic merchants, some
mere burden bearers! Mexico was always vulnerable and
outside events affected it. Vicissitudes of nature constantly
racked it and at least twice it was swallowed up by the
lake. As a people the Mexica were openly anxious and
feared time with its pulverizing and erosive strength.
Change and reversals were constantly poured out over this
city, altering its face. It was always aware of the possibility
of annihilation.

In layout and architecture the cities were distinctive and
seemed to belong to worlds apart. One obvious difference
was Mexico's lacustrine setting, yet perhaps even more
fundamental were each city's security measures.

In accordance with Peruvian custom Cuzco had a
pucara, a hilltop refuge. All the people of the Peruvian
highlands, whether organized in cantons or cities, possessed their pucara, the more inaccessible the better.
Generally it was protected either by man-made parapets
or natural precipices; in some of the more striking cases
walls within walls added to the defensive strength. Cuzco
was fortunately situated in that its pucara was right at its
back door, rising on the heights which closed the base of
the sacred triangle. This massive edifice, Sacsahuaman,
has already been mentioned. The interesting feature of
this fortress was that in all its pre-Spanish history Cuzco
never had occasion to use it.

The fortifications of Sacsahuaman clearly revealed this
ostentation for they were far more grandiose than was

necessary. Sacsahuaman was a showpiece; true, it was used as an armory and duly garrisoned, but it was principally intended to make manifest the untouchability of the sacred city below. No Incas probably ever thought that they might someday really need their pucara. Vastly impressive as a fortification, it was nevertheless primarily a statement of power.

Mexico on the contrary was defended naturally by its situation on an island. The three major causeways leading out to it were pierced at numerous places, and these spots bridged with planking which could be removed at need. Where the southern causeway from Ixtapalapan entered the city, a castle with two flanking towers barred the way. This was the nearest thing to a breastwork possessed by Mexico. The real reliance of the city was first in its vast canoe fleet (which could act offensively as well as defensively) and secondly, in the narrowness of the approaches. The city armory, according to Aztec custom, was included in the central temple area. It is true that those Aztec cities which were not built in the water, in many instances possessed formidable palisades and other fortifications. But in the main they appear to have defended themselves as open sites and thus were held with more tenacity than the Peruvian cities and towns, the inhabitants of which could always be vacated for greater safety to the pucara (in some cases miles away).

Being pinched in on a ridge between two swift and channeled streams, the city of Cuzco was otherwise undefended. It was composed of great *canchas* which were architecturally developed enclosures or yards, each devoted to the members of one extended Inca family. The high walls surrounding each yard were of stones meticulously fitted together and pierced generally by one portal only, narrow and easily supervised. Within each cancha were thatched villas and sets of apartments, corresponding in elaborateness to the status of the family holding it. The palace of the ruling monarch was simply another cancha though on a labyrinthine scale. The focal enclosure of the city was called Coricancha or "The Golden Yard"; this belonged to the family of the gods, each one of whom had his own thatched house backed up against the inside of the surrounding wall.

Huacaypata was the great square of Cuzco. It was the place where the Inca lords carried on their impressive cults and where they also held their prolonged carousals. Spacious but gloomy sheds lined the sides and provided cover in bad weather. The square was bare, unconnected with the temple area and was familial rather than public in most of its uses. None but Incas could move through it or otherwise inhabit it. It was holy ground not because of the near presence of gods and temples but because there fronted it the palatial canchas of the great Inca emperors, each of whom was a child of the sun.

The larger of the two Mexican islands, Tenochtitlan, markedly differed in this respect. Here the vast open square, the *teopantli*, was filled with temples and other sacred buildings scattered about seemingly at random. These included priestly quarters, sacramental tanks and bathing places, altars, armories, retreats, and skull-racks. The whole extent was surrounded by a wall pierced by four gates, one on each side, and was conceived as a *temenos*, an area sacred to the gods. The palaces of the rulers were outside the area and separated from its walls by eloquently empty spaces. However sacred Cuzco may have been, it still belonged wholly to the Inca caste. Mexico, as seen in the siting of the teopantli, belonged to the gods, and this in spite of the fact that it was a true city whereas Cuzco was not.

Of the two Mexico was the more beautiful. It lay placidly out in the waters, fringed with always verdant chinampas and isolated pleasure villas springing out of lush cane beds. Numerous temple pyramids, some of great height, towered everywhere over the city. Canals crowded with canoes penetrated into all areas and were more important than the roads and walkways. The houses of the nobles were painted bright colors and stood on raised terraces. The palaces were straggling edifices and had areas of superimposed quarters—comfortable esplanades connecting these second stories. From them one could take in a magnificent view, particularly eastward to the green shores across the many miles of the lake. There could be seen many allied cities and, as a backdrop to them, rose the solemn sierra ending with Popocatepetl in the south. In comparison Cuzco was huddled down in a valley and while its extraordinary thatches, heavily rounded and handsome, were unusual, the overall impression of the city was of a mere rearrangement, a ponderous reordering of the earth itself. Mexico was a picture of bright activity wholly man-made.

3

Wars and Premonitions of Empire

(1)

I used to believe that empire could be explained as a political vagary resulting from man's warlike disposition. I no longer do. I think, if anything, it is much more the reverse—that large-scale imperial warfare is simply a necessary fruit of empire, that what comes first is the acquisition of dominion over strangers, after which the technology of battle is widely and ingeniously expanded to maintain the dominion already seized.

But for a people that has not yet acquired an empire, war results from a state of apprehensiveness, a suspicion that neighbors will cast it under the yoke. Preimperial war comes from the unsleeping suspicion of these neighbors' intentions. Like many other peoples of history, Incas and Mexica both passed through this chrysalis stage of empire.

Having established themselves in their respective cities, Incas and Mexica spent the first years of their histories in often desperate involvements with the surrounding peoples. The Mexica, owing to their intransigence, had called into being a great coalition of cities against them and ended by becoming subject to the Tepanecas, powerful mainland people; they paid tribute by assisting in their masters' wars of imperial aggression. The Incas at a corresponding stage bit and scratched and cringed while waiting for their great chance. In the process both nations grew steadily and, indeed, ominously, enduring much and making some advances in the military arts.

In both instances the situation finally jelled and a significant step forward was taken under the threat of annihilation from the outside. Danger in the shape of an enemy at the gates was thus the key to their later destiny; in the case of the Incas it was the Chanca attack about 1438, and in the case of the Mexica it was the Tepaneca attack in 1427. In both cases success hung in the balance, and it may well have been the hairbreadth quality of the final deliverance which provided that élan in the national psyche impelling the two peoples toward adventures into empire.

There is no need here to detail the events of the two wars except to note that they both took their beginnings out of a deficiency of leadership. Viracocha Inca, for all his great talents, had become too old and besotted to ward off the Chanca menace. Chimalpopoca in Mexico fatuously involved himself in a conspiracy directed against his Tepaneca overlords without adequate precautions or backing from his own people. He ended his days caged up like an animal and dying of hunger and thirst, whereas Viracocha Inca abandoned his city and fled to an eyrie in the mountains.

Thus a vacuum in leadership had appeared among these two remarkable people at the very moment of their greatest danger. The events that followed form a similar and fascinating passage in pre-Columbian history.

As the formidable Chanca warriors moved down upon Cuzco, a supreme genius and leader of men miraculously appeared among the Incas. His full name was Cusi Inca Yupanqui but he is better known to us by his throne name Pachacuti. He was one of the sons of the emperor who had just fled leaving Cuzco undefended and quaking before the enemy onrush. By some miracle of leadership and with only the remnants of a nation around him, Pachacuti warded off the blow and eventually mounted a counterattack which sent the Chancas reeling back in confusion. In that instant the Inca empire as we know it was born, for the Inca armies from that time on never stopped advancing.

(2)

The Chanca crisis is focal in our understanding of Inca history. The monolithic quality of Inca history, its talent for a single-minded and overmastering policy, its insistence on autocratic unity, and its awesome administrative genius are surely the product of this one man. The Incas up to this point had been little different from any other ambitious and hectoring Peruvian people. They were resolute but nothing in their record foreshadowed their later greatness. Credit for that must be given to Pachacuti.

He was surely a frightening person, as formidable to the Incas as to their enemies, and the much misused designation "charismatic" can be applied to him with accuracy. The list of his deeds is legion and when he came to die he had recast the Inca state and created a true empire.

Historians today have discredited the hero theory of history. This is unfortunate, for while the theory does not explain the constant permutations of nations as they move about in their locked circles, endlessly appearing and endlessly disappearing, it does explain many features of sudden change. A hero in history is a man at whose appearance time loses its mastery of events, ceases to be a thing *sui generis,* and subserviently takes on the color and quality of the great man himself.

Necessarily this great man is a conqueror but he is almost always more than that. In his ingenuity and fancy he is a giant, performing exotic, unexpected, even totally unneeded deeds. It is generally lesser men who perform the deeds which the times have been calling for. The hero does not answer time's queries. He himself creates compelling new views and questions which, upon his passing, time carries about as if groaning under a burden.

Pachacuti was such a man. He was the greatest Amerindian in history and his mere presence is what gives Inca civilization its flavor.

Thus the Chanca crisis provided the opportunity for the Inca state to emerge from its chrysalis. And in elucidating the post-Chanca world of the Incas we are really describing the lengthened shadow of one individual. This must be constantly borne in mind.

Pachacuti ordered the rebuilding of Cuzco. He personally designated the huacas on each of the forty-one ceques, or invisible lines of force, leading out from Cuzco. He not only redid the central shrine in Cuzco, wrapping it in gold, but he redefined the authority of Inti himself, designating him now as a kind of surrogate for the newly installed high god and creator, Viracocha. He ordered the rewriting of history to conform to the Incas' new prestige. He made a pilgrimage to Pacaritambo to authenticate once and for all the divine origin of the Incas. He conquered far and wide and opened up to intensive exploitation the trans-Andean *montaña.* He conceived a network of wonderfully engineered roads. He created a whole new order of nobility to compensate for the defections and losses of the

Chanca war. He instituted a new principle of legitimacy in the royal family by marrying the heir-apparent to a full sister. He strengthened the succession, redid the ceremonial calendar, redefined and reconstituted the Inca ayllus, and finally expanded—if he did not create—the system of royal *panacas,* or the dead ruler's household, certainly among mankind's most curious inventions.

All of the above notable achievements were not necessarily without precedent, but it was Pachacuti's volcanic energy that drew them together into a complete formulation of empire.

(3)

Against this the Mexica picture looks diffuse, less radical, more haphazard. The reason is not hard to discern. No single overpowering personality arose to fill the power vacuum left by the death of Chimalpopoca. Victory in the Tepaneca war and the new political and international formulations following were the work of a collegiate body of knights, chief among whom were Itzcoatl, the elected ruler, and his two gifted nephews, Moteuczoma and Tlacaelel. The influence of these leaders and their immediate kinsmen lasted from 1427 to the death of Tlacaelel in the latter part of the century.

Taken together, the work of these three in some respect parallels that of Pachacuti. Here is a list of their activities to compare with those of the great Inca leader: repulse of the enemy attack and the followup drive to total victory; the first vision of empire; the creation of a new nobility; the building of new causeways across the lake; the rewriting of history; and the establishment of a special principle of succession. These were all major formulations and together they constituted a historical experience broadly similar to that of the Incas under Pachacuti. The fact of Mexican collegiality, however, puts a gloss upon this similarity which, when properly read, effectively reduces its impact. The collegiality we are referring to is best seen in the formidable and stifling presence among all the Aztec peoples of certain knightly orders inherited from the past.

These orders of knights (chief among which were the Eagles and Jaguars) could be traced back to similar associations among the earlier Toltecs. These sodalities provided opportunities for a man to acquire fame and their prestige was correspondingly enormous. The orders were not, as I have pointed out, the creations of the new state and, in some cases, they even stood opposed to its interests. It is important to realize that they were international in scope; every Aztec city had them. They represented what in effect was a single, international cult-oriented community interpenetrating all of the Aztec city-states. Their objectives were defined by an antique myth and not by the policy of any one state.

This myth was common to the whole of the Aztec world. It defined the sun as the paradigm of all valiant warriors and made plain that his daily fare consisted of the hearts and the blood of warriors killed in the course of their calling, either on the battlefield or as war captives sacrificed on the altar. It was insisted that without such fare the sun would weaken and falter in his daily round. The inference from this dogma was that the need to maintain a constant state of war had priority over the legitimate self-interest of the state.

This made vacillation and uncertainty in the aims of the Mexican state inevitable. The empire which Mexico carved for herself was consequently of a primitive variety for it could not control other competing interests. The warriors' need to display their individual valor often came first, whether this aided or impeded the growth of empire.

The Inca knights, on the contrary, were warriors trained in the tradition of fighting only for the defense or aggrandizement of the ayllu. Originally they had no loyalties larger than those to lineage or moiety. When their ranks were replenished by Pachacuti after his Chanca victory, these warriors were straitly and successfully tied into his imperialist plans. Their earlier allegiances were now transferred to the state and its empire, newly evolving under Pachacuti. By the end of Inca history they were the unquestioned policemen of the empire.

I am concerned lest this be misunderstood. In writing the above I mean to distinguish a variation in emphasis between the Aztec *teuctli* and the Inca *auca,* not a difference in kind. Like all good American Indian braves, both classes were put through typical initiation procedures stressing their impetuosity and endurance. The rites differed but the end product was the same, a man tied to a code of warfare and its attendant virtues. The difference between the teuctli and the auca is that the first was locked in an ancient and previous allegiance and thus could not always be used as the state desired. The teuctli lived two lives, the first one for the warrior sun-god, the other for the state.

The results were administratively impressive. Whereas the Inca state moved easily in an imperial direction at the command of one man, Mexico stumbled into independent empire and did not at any point pursue it as the supreme end of the state. The rulers of the Mexican state were themselves members of the knightly orders and thus they also had a double vision. The appearance of a hero in Inca

culture made possible the monolithic quality of Tahuantinsuyo; the presence of a set of knightly peers in Mexico
produced a less constricted, more open-ended history.

(4)

Battle was accordingly a different experience in the two
cultures and nothing else so clearly differentiates the two.
Let us analyze Inca warfare first.

The Inca knight, as I have stated, belonged in no special
category except insofar as he shared full malehood with
others in his ayllu. All Incas were peers because all were
warriors in the service of the community, at first the ayllu,
then the city, then Cuzcoquiti, the nuclear area surrounding Cuzco, then Tahuantinsuyo, the empire. When assigned to the command of tributary contingents these
warriors acted essentially as an officer class. There appear
to have been successive levels of command. The only
nonmilitary difference among these officers was their
affiliation with either Upper or Lower Cuzco.

When the emperor or his legate embarked on a
campaign, he was accompanied by what we can appropriately call the "Old Guard." This body was composed
of two regiments, one of Lower and one of Upper Cuzco.
Membership in these two cadres, both rank and file and
officers as well, was tantamount to an undisputed claim to
membership in an Inca ayllu. These regiments acted as a
strategic reserve, a shock body of veterans, and a personal
bodyguard for the emperor. On any major adventure they
were the heart of the army, thoroughly reliable, skilled,
and—because of their Inca blood—absolutely committed to
the commander-in-chief. Accounts have come down to us
of the incredible staying power of these troops.

These two regiments surrounded the emperor on the march and in the attack. Grouped around them were the bulk of the tributary conscripts officered by Incas acting through the local chiefs. The size of the army fluctuated according to the objective to be attained. The magnificent road system and the high degree of readiness of the local levies generally brought success.

In other words, the Inca concept of an army was something like ours today. It was viewed as a tool by which to achieve imperial aims. It existed for the state. War was therefore one of the styles adopted by Cuzcoquiti first to expand itself into empire and secondly to police this new order. War was nothing in itself. It only took on meaning as the state opted for it. War situations therefore arose only when a people refused to knuckle under to the threat of Inca power. Battle was joined to dislodge the enemy from his defenses and then killing or scattering sufficient numbers to force the rest into surrender.

Aztec warfare—and Mexica warfare spectacularly— existed *per se.* In a very real sense it was an activity unconnected with the state. Warfare was a divinely ordained institution and had been given to the Mexica as a mandate even before they founded their city. In other words, war preceded the state, which is why at any time thereafter it could occur with no references to the state's intentions.

War need not be a political or even an imperial activity among the Aztecs. It was often a cult act and those who tended the cult and saw to its proper service were essentially priests. This is not to say that the Aztec warrior did not relish war, as his Inca counterpart did, or derive reputation and honors from it. He did, but he had also taken vows in a cosmic cause and he was thus never free from the overriding purpose of the cult which was the shedding of human blood so the gods could feast and fatten.

It regularly happened in Mexico that the mighty earth goddess, speaking through omens for all the rest of the gods, would suddenly announce the divine hunger and thirst. Regardless of the international position of the state at that moment or regardless of any considerations for its security, contingents would be thereupon dispatched on raids or on tournaments purposely arranged with other Aztec states, which coincidentally also might be requiring an effusion of blood. These tournaments were specially designated as "flower-wars" and were the particular pride of the knightly orders. It did not really matter which side prevailed—from the cosmic point of view that is; what counted was the number of captives taken (who would later be sacrificed to the gods) and the numbers of one's own side killed or lost to the enemy. No discrimination was made as to whether the blood of the enemy stained your altars or the blood of your own men flowed on the field or on sacrificial stones in the cities of the enemy. To be able to carry out their functions the gods presiding over the universe needed sustenance; either victory or defeat fed them equally well.

In the melee the Aztec warrior strove to cover himself with glory, for exceptional valor assured him a place in the sun-god's entourage after his death. The heart of a coward or a sluggard in war was tasteless to the gods. Battle therefore tended among the Aztecs to be a set of personal duels and war was simply the enlarged opportunity for the warrior to engage in many such contests.

Occasionally the expansionist program of the state did coincide with the hunger of the gods. Then the armies marched with brilliant gains to be made and twofold successes possible, one for the heavens and one for the earth. The state occasionally could be the beneficiary of a cosmic situation.

This Aztec concept of war would produce a radically different empire than Tahuantinsuyo, the Four Quarters of the Inca world.

4

The New States

(1)

As the Inca and the Mexica emerged from their initial crises into an unfamiliar world of decisions and responsibilities, they both found themselves with governments much too rudimentary for their needs. It was important that they adopt constitutions which would correspond to the new duties thrust upon them.

The fact that one of the cultures had produced a hero who singlehandedly guided the state through the transitional period to empire whereas the other achieved its purposes by collegiality, determined that the shape of the two emergent states should be dissimilar. The Inca state as refashioned was dogmatic, monarchical, and exclusive; it existed for its own purposes, or—which is much the same thing—for the purposes of the emperor. The Mexican state became an institution whose policy was captive to the overriding cult of war, and it thus took on the appearance of an engine very often supportive of a class of knights whose aims were international and/or cosmic, certainly not solely statist. To the modern viewer the Inca state has clear and unchallengeable outlines; the Mexican state constantly eludes definition.

The new imperial office filled by Pachacuti and his successors grew out of an earlier and common Peruvian office known as that of the *sinchi,* the "strong man," a relatively undifferentiated and originally elective office filled only in times of crisis. Its final evolutionary transformation into the office of *capac apu Inca,* the "magnificent Inca prince," was the direct result of the memorable victory over the Chancas. In other words, the potential uniqueness of the office had been historically enlarged and validated. The only real problem was to be the relationship between this sole Inca, the "sapay Inca," and all other Incas.

Pachacuti's solution to this potentially dangerous problem was threefold: first, an expansion and therefore something of a dilution of the whole caste of Incas; second, a fragmentation and insulation of the old Inca families into *panacas* (which will be explained below); and third, the harnessing and taming of Inca energies in planned and unremitting warfare and tours of administration.

The expansion of the Inca class was made necessary because of the desertions and attrition experienced during the Chanca war. Needless to say, Incas claimed an elite status, superior to that of all other peoples, and this had on all accounts to be maintained as the underpinning of the monarchy. Therefore Pachacuti turned his attention first to receiving into Inca ranks those notable chieftains and their immediate subordinates who had risked much in offering their services to him in the supreme crisis of the state. A vast scheme of marriages was instituted to perpetuate this new nobility which now gave Pachacuti a lever to use, whenever needed, against older and more stubborn Inca families.

These older families had had their powers of resistance to the new imperial institutions neatly clipped when Pachacuti renovated the panaca, which was the household of a dead ruler. Because there had been eight rulers, beginning with Manco Capac and coming down through Pachacuti's predecessor and father, there were therefore eight of these ancestral cults existing at the time (actually there were nine as Pachacuti's own family counted as a panaca and would continue so to act after his death). These were now remade into households wherein the dead ruler, either a mummy or a crude stone effigy, was treated in every way as if he were alive and still carrying on his rule. The older and more prestigious Incas were assigned to various of these households or were allowed to elect membership in any one they preferred. Each of these households was assigned a cancha in Cuzco within whose walls a full round of activities was carried on by the dead ruler and his servitors. Just as if he were alive he was carried about in a litter and attended public events; he was fed, he visited others, or he offered drinking bouts to outside panacas. What made this curious system viable was the fact that an emperor's wealth on his demise was not passed on to his heir; inasmuch as he was considered to be still in some sense alive, the disposition of his wealth had as always to remain in his own hands. Thus, what was in one sense an ancestor cult in another was a way of enticing into luxurious but sterile activities the most important—and therefore the most potentially dangerous —living members of the Inca caste.

With the panaca as a political opiate for his own people, Pachacuti used constant warfare to dampen potential revolt among his more warlike subjects. Conquered groups known for their aggressiveness or suspected of lack of loyalty were always heavily taxed in terms of numbers of fighting men for use in the Inca armies. A numerous subcaste of bastard Incas was correspondingly made into a professional class of what we might call noncommissioned officers whose duty was to train and supervise those warlike subjects; both officers and men were generally stationed far from Cuzco on garrison duty or on campaign. Others of these bastard Incas were siphoned off into administration in the provinces.

This carefully worked out expansion, inoculation, and distribution of the energies of his people gave to the office of *capac apu Inca* some security against conspiracy or insurrection. Nor did the office of high priest pose any threat to him, for it was strictly ecclesiastical and was always held by a trusted relative.

As for the state itself it is possible to define it geographically; it was more than the capital city, being in fact the large and productive area surrounding Cuzco called Cuzcoquiti. This nuclear state had accurately defined borders and included the inner, compacted area in which the early Incas had once battled against and subjugated their neighbors. Technically Cuzcoquiti was not a part of the empire; it was more like the suburban territory of a city-state. Into it had been brought numerous groups of the conquered as a work force which, having come from far places, would not easily acquire a vested interest in the new fields. Cuzcoquiti was thus a polyglot area in the heart of the empire. Mass marriages were arranged between these people and the loyal subjects to further weaken their social ties and extraneous loyalties. Cuzcoquiti in short was a well-run economic state, the lynchpin and basic territorial center of Tahuantinsuyo.

(2)

The ruler of Mexico was a *tlatoani*, a "speaker" or "one who gives commands." It is probable but not certain that the office was originally that of a war chief. Beside this office and of almost equal weight was that of the *cihuacoatl,* a word which means "snake-woman" and is the prime name of the Aztec earth-goddess. Whereas the tlatoani was the chief executive, the cihuacoatl might more properly be called the head of state.

This needs some explanation, for like all analogies it is not quite exact. The Mexican state, as we have noted, existed on two planes, or rather it existed for two purposes, one political, the other cosmic. On the one hand it existed for its own ends such as security, aggrandizement, and jurisdiction. On the other it existed to serve the cosmic order, its designated role here being the maintenance of the cult of blood. The tlatoani ruled the state if we think of it as a political community, the cihuacoatl ruled the state if we consider it to have been primarily a religious community.

The cihuacoatl's power was founded in his control of the "Great Mother's" oracles. Hers was the most authentic of all the divine voices and spoke through him, demanding the gods' due in blood and hearts or scolding the state for being dilatory in providing the same. At such times orders would immediately be issued by the tlatoani for an outpouring of knights. Thereby the tlatoani gave up his right to make independent decisions in the interests of the state and became merely the organizer of a sacramental act. Needless to say there were other occasions where the tlatoani did act in full sovereignty and from considerations of state policy. There could be, however, no occasions where wills clashed. The oracles of Cihuacoatl took precedence over any royal dictum.

There was a further restriction on the tlatoani. There sat with him on all major decisions an inner council of four great princes, all of them nearly related. Their power was real for they had been elected at the same time as the tlatoani and it would be they who would choose his successor from among themselves when he left the scene. The tlatoani in brief was the first among five peers.

Behind this inhibitory system can be seen the lineaments of a fantastic class of nobles, the *teuctlis.* These were the lords esteemed not only because of their birth (a high desideratum), but because of their attainments in war or in the councils. The bulk of them were coopted into the knightly orders and, once enrolled, acquired an autonomy that overrode the authority of the state and only coincided with it when, in response to oracles, the state entered upon a war that coincidentally served its own interests.

Now, when it is realized that both the tlatoani and the cihuacoatl were themselves raised as teuctlis and unquestioningly accepted their values, it can be seen that this is a description of a state and constitution possessing very limited options, one forced willy-nilly into constant war. Inasmuch as all other Aztec states accepted the same limitations, Mexico does not appear to have been particularly weak. But weak it was, if judged in terms of its freedom to maneuver politically. This weakness is most clearly seen in the events that attended the irruption of the Spaniards.

The new nobility created by Itzcoatl at the conclusion of the Tepaneca war is in no way comparable to the new Incas ennobled by Pachacuti. The latter were raised up with the full realization that their whole allegiance was to the *capac Inca* and to him alone. The postwar Mexican teuctli, newly knighted, was simply the augmentation of a momentarily depleted class—and this class carried with it ancient prerogatives of warring in the interests of the gods. The Mexican state supinely accepted this.

A final criterion of the limited nature of the tlatoani's

office can been in the fact of his mortality. The Inca ruler never died nor did he give up his wealth and daily service—the panaca was a fortress of his ever-continuing sovereignty. No such institution existed among the Aztecs. Like any other nobleman, the tlatoani was cremated, his soul ascended into the heavens to accompany the sun, and at the last, after four years in the sun's retinue, he became a butterfly or a bird.

The Incas were able to produce a consolidated territorial state (Cuzcoquiti) far larger than Cuzco itself and supportive of it. Mexico remained a city in a lake; the lands held outside Mexico by the various calpullis, temples, rulers, and nobles were scattered about without reference to territorial unity. There was nothing therefore which corresponded to Cuzcoquiti.

(3)

Aristocracy and the state, whenever they coexist in a historical framework, work out what is at best a precarious *modus vivendi;* where the nobility serves the state there is more directed energy available and a greater effectiveness. We have seen that from Pachacuti on (with one important exception during the reign of Huayna Capac) the Incas were tamed, molded, and cajoled into doing the imperial will. They thus became in great part personnel adapted to administrative work. The Mexican aristocracy, on the contrary, basing its claims on its Toltec blood, successfully withstood all attempts in the early and middle periods of Aztec history to reduce its influence. It could do this because it filled what was essentially a sacramental office.

But at the end of Mexican history—and very unexpectedly—the powers of this group of men were curtailed and for a while it appeared that a true sovereignty would arise on the erosion of their prerogatives. The man who almost brought this about was Moteuczoma, second of the name and the one commonly and erroneously referred to in our literature as Montezuma. A brief glance at this passage in Mexican history will be enlightening.

Moteuczoma II was elected in 1503 because of his high lineage, his excellent war record, his sententiousness, and his dignity. Nobility and legitimate birth were matters of moment to every teuctli, but Moteuczoma displayed an inflated pride in his lineage which surprised even his close supporters. Immediately upon his election he revised the entire court protocol (including the educational system for the sons of the nobility) with such precipitation and cold fury as to horrify the capital city. His predecessor had employed able commoners around him wherever he had felt the need. These people were now summarily dismissed by Moteuczoma and even in some cases liquidated. A concomitant order went out that all illegitimate sons of noblemen being at that moment trained in the academies should be immediately dismissed. This purification of the teuctli ranks had the curious consequence of also demoting them at the same time, for by upgrading the social purity of the class supporting the tlatoani, his own standing was even further enhanced. Many of the legitimate sons of the nobles were now called into court service as pages, to perform the menial services for Moteuczoma formerly entrusted to commoners and the lesser nobility.

As long as Moteuczoma lived, this reduction in the standing of the nobles vis-à-vis the tlatoani was maintained, and had Mexican history continued it can be argued that this development would have been stressed even more, eventuating finally in the creation of an absolute monarchy as in the Inca case. I can see, however, certain objections to this speculation, not the least being one taken from the international environment in which the Aztec cities were immersed.

(4)

The international and intertribal worlds into which the Inca and Aztec states were born differed markedly. The Incas themselves were *sui generis;* they owned to having no relatives, no predecessors, and—what is very questionable—no allies. They fought their way up as one among several competing but unrelated states in the great Peruvian altiplano. This made transition from a conglomeration of hamlet-dwellers to absolute monarchy easy, for there was a premium upon any group that could most easily produce and implement a policy. And it was in this particular that the Incas excelled. Thus their cultural environment—external as well as internal—fostered integration of the instruments of rule, the result in their case being the office of the *capac Inca,* paramount and untrammeled.

The Mexican matter was different, for the roots of this people stood deep in the springs of the whole Aztec world, which was itself a post-Toltec civilization. In this world of peers the Mexica were known to be the youngest and therefore the least likely to depart from the norm. The story of Aztec civilization as a whole was the story of protracted and always frustrated attempts by the various cities to achieve supremacy. Mexico simply followed their lead.

For the survival of the Mexica in such a jostling and crowded world, accommodation and alliance were required. Thus they helped to create at the beginning of the Tepaneca war the famous Three-City League, comprising the states of Tezcoco, Mexico, and Tlacopan. With this international instrument, Mexico was to win success in the Aztec world but only as one of three partners. Each of the partners—if the League were to work—perforce had to accommodate somewhat to the others. That the League itself aspired to dominion over all of Mesoamerica is undoubted but its ultimate failure to do so proves that the Aztec milieu was more intractable than that of the Peruvian altiplano. All Aztec peoples spoke a common language, Nahuatl. And we have seen that each city-state was supported by a knightly class, the teuctlis. These two features ineluctably weakened the possibility that any Aztec state would rise to a dominant position. So Mexican history was played out linked in a pact with others, whereas the Incas performed their ruthless miracles alone.

This league factor in Mexican history at the very end did, however, begin to disintegrate as Mexico under Moteuczoma II succeeded in dividing Tezcoco and relegating Tlacopan to an inferior status. Thus it was that Mexico stood poised and ready to attempt singlehanded the rule of a consolidated empire, to do, in other words, what the Incas did—but at too late a date. The Spaniards were already knocking at the gates.

(5)

I have used the word "state" frequently in this chapter but I have done so with some trepidation and wishing there were a better term. Nuclear America was Neolithic in its technology and perhaps at a no later stage than that in its social orientation. It is obvious that states such as we know them today could not suddenly and wonderfully emerge out of such a matrix.

What the Incas and Mexica inherited from the past and partially reworked to their own specifications were indeed the most hazy of political constitutions. Add to this that the terrors and splendors of nature continued to afflict these peoples directly and sometimes dangerously—personified in the gods, nature was their ever-present enemy. They wandered about in a world of greatly unequal protagonists—pygmies versus giants, states versus gods. They were disturbed spirits and their political creations reflect this.

I think that I might go so far as to say that certainly the Mexican state and, in part, Tahuantinsuyo were substituting—in what looks to me like a political context—for the old Paleolithic shaman, doing his work of whistling to the winds, curing, speaking with ghosts, and piercing the suffocating veils of the divine. This interpretation of mine flies in the face of the archaeological theory that the Post-Classic period in Nuclear America was more secular than the previous Classic age. Perhaps I am putting the case too strongly but I do not think so.

In the matter of the Mexican state there can be no dispute about its fundamental attunement to the world of the spirit. A critic might well take exception, however, to my insistence that the Inca state was also a spiritual constitution. But what then will that critic say to the organization of the city of Cuzco as a primary dispensing point of the power of huaca? What will he say about the fact that Tahuantinsuyo could not take shape until a god was raised up great enough to care for it? What can he say to the enervating fear the late Incas had of the god's return? Of the fact that ceremonialism was the very language of the state? Or of the spiritualistic orgy indulged in by Huascar as the imperial tale ended? And indeed what can this critic say to the final confession in 1572 of Tupac Amaru at the Spanish chopping block, where this last claimant to the Inca throne admitted that he and his predecessors had manipulated cult for the needs of the state?

The Inca state, Cuzcoquiti, and its empire, Tahuantin-suyo, were more rationally conceived than the Mexican state and empire, but neither in fact belong to the rational tradition. They were constructions of such an antique frame of mind that we find it difficult to perceive that in one deep sense they were similar. Both acknowledged the tendency—and even the intent—of the gods to destroy them.

5

The Outer Faces of the Empires

(1)

It is obvious that empire did not suddenly occur to our two peoples. However different their apprenticeships to empire appear to us in details, they are alike in the gradualism by which the imperial idea appeared in their histories.

The Inca drift toward empire was relatively uncomplicated. By the reign of Inca Roca, the sixth ruler, the state of Cuzco was viable and had made its mark. Petty wars and raids had filled Cuzco's days up to then, but at that point a new group of captains was appearing whose outstanding energy carried Inca arms over the high ridges and down into neighboring valleys. Yet this was still not imperial expansion because the peoples and hamlets forced to their knees were simply stripped bare—there was no attempt to organize the conquests and the raiders simply withdrew after each mission.

The plunder continued to enrich the little state as the captains became more skilled and soon the situation was ripe for a change. There finally appeared a ruler named Hatun Topa Inca (later to become Viracocha Inca). It was he who saw the possibilities of organizing future raids and conquests into an enduring pattern of subjection. What he saw was, as we now know, the possibility of empire. Cities and villages overcome in war were now garrisoned; instead of being then and there put to the sack, they were carefully preserved in their governments and resources with the important addendum that a portion of those resources was annually drawn off by Cuzco.

Note the Mexican case. After their defeat at Chapultepec and their subsequent schism into two groups, the Mexica served under Tezozomoc, the stern Tepaneca taskmaster, who was at that time striving for imperial jurisdiction over the Aztec world. In this fast-moving, experimental context the Mexica were consciously trained in the arts of imperial war. Their contribution as warriors was the tribute they paid to Tezozomoc, for as a people living in the midst of waters their natural resources were limited.

Though they became more and more deeply involved in the military search for empire, it was still the planning and vision of others, namely their masters, the Tepaneca, which guided them. As time passed and their facility in war was sharpened, they increasingly were allowed to exercise dominion over Aztec cities they had helped to conquer. Thus what they were in the act of gaining was not a classic empire such as Tahuatinsuyo was, but rather a kind of subempire which was theirs only through a process of subinfeudation.

When Tezozomoc (under whom the Mexica were acquiring this empire) died his successor instantly cancelled all Mexican holdings and prepared to reduce the Mexica again to a bare level of subsistence. At this juncture the cities of Mexico, Tezcoco, and Tlacopan created the alliance that finally crushed the new Tepaneca tyrant and suddenly cast them in the role of arbiters of the

Mesoamerican world. Now for the first time Mexico could enjoy a period of empire-building in an independent capacity, sovereign yet indissolubly bound by a three-way treaty obligation to march with allies, fight with them, and divide with them the spoils and prestige acquired in war.

Thus began the so-called Aztec empire. In reality it was three empires held respectively by three sovereign states of which Mexico was only one. The ambitious Mexica had not planned it that way—the exigencies of their struggle for independence had necessitated it. The Incas conceived of empire as the conscious and total policy orientation of one sovereign state; the Mexica, travelling a different historical road, could not see it thus.

(2)

Once acquired—whether by design or accident—empire has to be organized and defined. The Incas saw their empire as an administrative responsibility; the Mexica looked upon theirs as loot. The two viewpoints created greatly contrasting empires.

I am not here preferring one to the other. In the brutality with which they pursued their ends there was no difference between the two; in the Amerindian world there was no ideological background which would enable a state to understand a moral commitment to other peoples. The calculated and cold-blooded terrorism of the Incas created the same abject grovelling and desperation in those under them as did the berserker ferocity of the Mexica. What I am really saying is that Tahuantinsuyo is an empire more easily understood by us today for it had careful outlines and was in part a rational structure. The

Mexica empire lacked precisely those characteristics. The distinction can be best seen in the matter of roads, posts, and language.

I said that Tahuantinsuyo was in part a rational structure and this means that its parts were bound together with care and intelligence. The road system constructed by the Incas has ranked, ever since Pizarro first landed in Peru, as one of the wonders of the world, and this with good reason. In the variety, elegance, and permanence of its engineering it is indeed superb, but in the conception that lay behind it, it is even more masterly. This conception is that of the world as a highway in spite of all natural signs to the contrary.

I here admit to infinite wonder. The altiplano on which the Incas carried out their bold design is not, as cheap topographical maps would have us believe, an elongated, elevated, and continuous plateau between the Andes on the east and the Sierra Occidental on the west. It is cut with stupendous gorges and sometimes blocked by heavy knots of mountains. To live on the altiplano is not to automatically adapt to a natural and continuous north-south arrangement of arterial traffic. Sudden and stupifying contrasts in temperature, humidity, and air density were an ordinary part of the adventure of travelling this highway. Only a people convinced of the easy assailability of all parts of the world and of their mission to force their way into these parts could have thought of the altiplano as a highway.

To pierce the great crumpled walls on either side, feeder roads dropped down from the mountain axis into either the wild montaña, the gold and coca country, on the east, or, on the west, into the sandy areas of the coast, rich, ancient, and sophisticated. All of these roads were paved and interconnected; they carried easily the stores and armies of the empire, but even more spectacularly they carried its messages.

The *chasqui* system was a model of efficiency and organization; it was manned, as part of their annual tribute to Cuzco, by the tribes and peoples through which the roads ran. Young and tough-winded runners, picked for their ability in racing relays of about four miles each, passed messages along at top speed regardless of weather or steepness of grade. Cuzco was well over a thousand miles from Quito, yet it took on the average only six days for information to travel the distance. Messages, shouted from runner to runner, pacing beside each other, were confirmed at the receiving end by the knotted cords (*quipus*) of colored strings they carried, which had been also passed along and which had numerical and allusive meanings.

The *chasquis* and the roads they ran on are a sufficient explanation for the great spread of the Inca empire. From north to south this empire stretched for well over twenty-five hundred miles. The Incas saw clearly the connection between speed in communication and the stability and extent of an empire. Aware of this connection they created the appropriate institutions.

Because of the contrasting nature of their empire the Mexica saw no such connection. They never thought of their irregular and widely flung empire as an area for the exercise of administrative techniques which would promote order and predictability. Indeed they saw no particular value in these latter aspects of rule, for they knew the gods to be excessively whimsical, allowing no people to achieve much in the realm of culture-building. If disorder and rebellion kept breaking out in their provinces so much the better, for the knights then could display their intrepidity on a new field of honor.

Whereas the Incas had organized a courier system covering most of their empire, we hear only of one Mexican post. This ran from their capital down through Orizaba to the provincial capital of Cotastla near the coast. On this route we hear of closely spaced post-stations and also some travellers' inns, but the way was not paved nor was it provided with culverts, tunnels, and steps as was the Capac Ñan, "the Great Road" of Peru. On the Aztec road messages were carried three hundred miles in a twenty-four-hour period, which is a rate fully comparable to the Inca achievement. It is possible—even probable—that this road served all three of the intermingled empires and thus was not wholly Mexican.

The reason why the Mexican empire was not tied together in a communications and road network is obvious. It was not a contiguous set of subject states and provinces but was rather interwoven with the disparate holdings of the other two allies in the league, Tezcoco and Tlacopan. The lack of centralization and unity militated against any need being felt by either of the three sovereign cities for a set of arterial roads utilized in common. Furthermore there were important enclaves of unsubjugated and hostile states within the greater area of the Aztec empire. Tahuantinsuyo moved methodically ahead absorbing all in its path. As it advanced it left no unconquered ethnic islands behind it to cloud the image of its unity.

(3)

In trade and warehousing there were also notable differences.

As one would expect in the case of an omnivorous

empire, Tahuantinsuyo either monopolized the important commodities on the altiplano or closely regulated them. Among the Mexica, trade had a life of its own, was organized in something like guilds and showed some characteristics of free enterprise. We often hear of famous merchants in Mexico by name, and the word for merchant, *pochtecatl,* has several variants, attesting to the antiquity of the profession.

The life of the Mexican pochtecatl comes down to us fully and vividly described in the sources. He was a man who inherited an immemorial skill and daring. In most ways his calling set him apart from the rest of his society. He was proud of himself and of his profession which entailed the maximum in endurance and was never without its perils.

References to commerce in the history of Tahuantinsuyo are rare. No merchants are known by name and there is no word in classical Quechua which gives the sense of a person who carries goods to far places, risking much to exchange them for other items. Commerce there was aplenty in Tahuantinsuyo but all luxury items such as coca and gold were imperial monopolies and moved about in llama-caravans under military escort and bureaucratic supervision. Guard points were placed at every bridge of consequence and in every strategic pass. At these places all goods were inspected to see if they were moving under license. Trade in the Inca empire was thus anonymous, constant, and peaceful; it involved only a modicum of risk.

It is difficult for us to distinguish legitimate trade here from the movement of tribute. In Tahuantinsuyo goods generally moved from the provincial capitals into warehouses in Cuzcoquiti via llama-back. Because in Mesoamerica there was no corresponding beast of burden to accelerate traffic, all goods were carried on the backs of porters, a special and hereditary class of men. Nor did the Aztec empire have a graded hierarchy of warehouses for ease of storage. Once on the move tribute—whether gold dust, colored feathers, or sacks of dried maize—had to keep going until deposited in the appropriate repository in Mexico.

Mexico lived in a world where commerce was an antique and dramatic adventure carried out by private individuals. The Mexican merchants in some cases carried goods belonging wholly to themselves—their risk being thus enormously increased. In other cases they traded partly in state-owned goods and had therefore the special backing of the tlatoani. There is an epic quality about the stories that come down to us concerning these Aztec entrepreneurs which is wholly lacking in the tight state-organized caravans of Tahuantinsuyo.

(4)

In nothing do our two empires differ so much as in the storage of goods, yet in both cases we feel the same wonderful greed of men newly released from the strait-ness of tribal living.

The Incas had the instincts of the pack-rat developed to the highest degree. Undoubtedly, the reason behind this mania for piling up surpluses was the unbelievably precarious existence of the Peruvian altiplano's dwellers; the necessity to store seed-potatoes and *quinoa* against the next unpredictable but certainly harsh season; and the doling out of carefully calculated stocks as the year wore to a close. Yet added to this was also an astute policy. By taxing their subject provinces to the extent of their whole surplus, the Incas insured their unremitting labor and thus reduced the incidence of revolt. By storing these surpluses in royal compounds in the provincial capitals, they created a cushion against local crisis and a reservoir upon which Cuzcoquiti could draw at any time.

Tribute naturally varied from province to province. Some handed over to their masters gold dust, some gave the service of royal litter bearers, some gave dried maize or potato flour (*chuño*), while others gave beautiful girls. All items were meticulously warehoused under bureaucratic control, and statements of contents and withdrawals sent to the central government. The system was designed not only to weaken the vigor of the subject people and thus reduce their potential role as troublers of the state, but also and primarily to emphasize the paternalism of the imperial government.

How vastly different was the Mexican case! Tribute was dispatched every eighty days (four Aztec months) by caravans of porters from each provincial capital to Mexico (and also to Tezcoco and Tlacopan from their own imperial provinces). Owing to the lack of warehousing in those provincial capitals no elaborate bureaucracy was needed. Everything was on a more primitive level and the tribute coming in was all stored directly in the armories, wardrobes, and granaries of Mexico. The Mexica lacked the quick computation system of the Incas (the *quipu*) and, while we have no doubt that their accounts on paper were surely as accurate as those of the Incas, they were not as sophisticated and as easily filed away. The Mexican system was essentially an immediate transfer of loot from the conquered to the conquerors; the Inca system was that plus a flexible instrument used to tighten imperial control. The Mexica preferred to garrison a province rather than to control it bureaucratically.

(5)

To the Incas empire was synonymous with order and an absence of disaffection. To the Aztecs empire was a byproduct of warfare and not a state objective; thus, to them their empire was not of paramount importance. These profound divergences created great administrative contrasts in their respective methods of rule.

Tahuantinsuyo was organized on a decurial system wherever practicable; each newly acquired province was divided into an ascending order of household groups, the basic group comprising ten households. Out of this group a member was appointed to act as agent of the imperial government, not only for purposes of gathering the proper tribute or information from the ten households, but also for passing orders down to them. Over every ten of these groups there was a centurion. Over ten centuries there was a leader of a thousand, and so on up.

This rational and autocratic scheme gave the Incas a remarkable hold over their subject peoples, perhaps most of all because of its efficiency in gathering and processing information. Allied to this was a system whereby elements of peoples who had long been under the Inca yoke and were therefore acclimatized to the system, were inserted into the villages and countryside of a province just organized. These transferred groups were called *mitmacs;* they acted as educators, language instructors, spies, and loyal elements to Tahuantinsuyo. They spoke Quechua and were supposed to spread the use of that imperial tongue, thus quickly binding the new province to the empire. Reciprocally, clusters of the conquered peoples—the more dangerous ones—were transferred hundreds of miles away to become permanent residents of far distant but somewhat similar areas. In their new homes, however, they retained their former tribal associations with those left behind, which further fragmented them and sterilized their capacities to foment trouble. The policy that lay behind the transplanting of peoples and the teaching of one common tongue was the desire to produce an amalgam of populations which would eventually change Tahuantinsuyo from an empire of conquest into a voluntary one. All of this reveals to us a bigness of conception on the part of the Incas and a familiarity in dealing with relatively sophisticated levels of empire.

To the Mexica, empire remained a form of plunder and they never evolved a method which would embody a sense of responsibility toward it. The more dynamic world of the battlefield and the sacrificial stone consumed too much of their devotion and all of their higher thoughts. Administration, with all of its tamping down of drama, would have interfered with their duties as bondsmen in a cosmic empire. The nearest they came to day-by-day control of their subjects was in the drastic instance when they dispossessed or liquidated the ruling house of a conquered people and installed military government. This was, however, simply evidence of the intransigence of those particular subjects and not a special instrument of rule on the part of the Mexica. There was nothing resembling the decurial system for purposes of imperial census and, while accounting techniques were on a par with those of the Incas, so far as we know they were used only for the registry of tribute and not for broader purposes of information and forecast. The Incas, trusting in their destiny as a master race, planned ahead whereas the Aztecs, pessimistic and acutely aware of irresponsibility as a main characteristic of the gods, lived from day to day dutifully performing the rites of war.

(6)

It may be of interest in analyzing more closely the two empires at their height to contrast the historical style of two of their rulers, Topa Inca and Axayacatl; those two are comparable because they both immediately followed the period of imperial formulation.

First of all we can see that there was no difference whatsoever in their warlike skills. The two men were remembered for successful and sometimes reckless military ventures and for the consequent great expansion of their respective empires. This was *de rigueur*. Both were also looked upon as models and were fully accepted into the canons of deserving rulers. Both were wholly legitimate as far as concerned their right to rule and thus both possessed the favor of the gods. From the above points of view, they could therefore be thought of as perfect rulers.

But how very different they were! Topa Inca's reign was a miracle of imperial reorganization, of supervisor activity, and of determined warfare. Axayacatl's reign was a miracle of personal heroism on the field of battle, of unsurpassed piety, and of brute daring.

Style in ruling may seem a somewhat nebulous concept—certainly it is difficult to gauge. However, if we define it as that set of personality traits which supplement policy, then it may be useful to apply here. Topa Inca's style was dedicated, gigantic, clearheaded; Axayacatl's style was personal, intense, and exemplary.

Topa Inca had been specially designated to the succession. He was reared in boyhood on campaigns by trusted generals and, coached by his stern father Pachacuti, he followed closely in those distinguished footsteps. As coregent he learned the hard ways of an imperial world through intrigues, conspiracies, and massive rebellions. He successfully put down a coalition of revolting Collas and Lupacas in the Titicaca area. At great cost Topa Inca pushed the empire farther up the spine of the Andes to gain Quito. He sent his armies down into the midst of the powerful coastal states and battered them into submission. He challenged the terrible montaña, gained new provinces there, notably Chachapoyas, and with cavalier disdain lost more than one army in those sucking fastnesses. He thrust his imperial grasp far down into Chile seeking new gold-producing areas. In brief, his vigor as an empire builder was boundless and his successes most notable.

As an administrator, Topa Inca appears to have surpassed his amazing father. He reorganized the whole Chucuito area after the Colla rebellion. Even though he operated through a delegative system, he kept a jealous control over all of his imperial prerogatives. He issued new laws and was known for his ability to command the whole extent of Tahuantinsuyo. He radically expanded the mythology upon which the empire rested by commandeering the famous highland shrines of Titicaca and Koati and incorporating them into the Inca world-view, reworking their tales and cults to support Inca pretensions to world dominance. He demoted uncooperative or competing shrines and he publicly insulted hostile gods. Topa Inca ended his days in a vast imperial progress which, for all those who cared to see, demonstrated the unshakable unity of Tahuantinsuyo.

Axayacatl was a prominent Mexican warrior and by reason mainly of that reputation was elected to the position of tlatoani. His coronation raid (to secure victims for his installation ceremonies) was a deep and audacious thrust into southern Guerrero and Tehuantepec. It proved his continuing dependability as a warrior and a leader of fighting men. His war record during his reign was therefore predictably distinguished; it included among others a violent and unprovoked assault upon the tough communities of Michoacán—this eventuating in a nearly total disaster for Mexico and a glorious shedding of blood. Most importantly he successfully withstood the treacherous attack delivered upon the Tenochca by their Mexican fellows on the northern island Tlatilulco. He cut that Gordian knot of Mexican history by placing Tlatilulco under a stern military government. Out of this victory appeared a new military orientation of Mexico pointing to the west, the conquest of the Toluca Basin and the upper Lerma drainage, and, finally, the abovementioned misadventure in Michoacan.

Axayacatl achieved the pinnacle of virtue when in furious battle he was captured, cruelly wounded in the thigh, and then recaptured. His piety was attested to by the splendor of his dedication of Huitzilopochtli's new temple, for in that ceremony some ten thousand hearts, torn out of the living bodies of as many captured warriors, were held aloft and offered to the gods. A large sun-stone, possibly the one now displayed in the Museo Nacional de Antropología, was erected to exposit the cosmological significance of all such events. Unfortunately we know nothing about Axayacatl's administrative abilities; the absence of any kind of comment may be an admission that in such endeavors he was not outstanding.

From this juxtaposition of careers clearly emerges the divergent imperial ambitions of the two peoples. In the case of Mexico the ruler was considered to be the incarnate spirit of the model warrior, who in turn was the officiant in the cult of war. He had to be this even before he displayed a matching ability in the adjustments, accommodations, and decisions necessary to the carrying on of daily affairs. Axayacatl may thus have represented the Mexican state, but he did not represent the Mexican empire. Topa Inca leaned heavily on the viceregal concept of government and thus personally represented the empire and its expansive needs—that is to say, he was less responsive to the expectations of his Inca peers, who made up the ruling class of the state, and more deeply involved in an individual enterprise taught to him by his father —the business of empire.

6

The Inner Faces of the Empires

(1)

The foregoing chapter has led us directly into the need to discover the underpinnings of the empires created by these two peoples. We will begin with the definition of an empire as something which a state creates and which —once created—has a tendency to turn upon the parent state, either consuming or altering it, in the process of which it becomes itself a derived state but one on a much different level and decidedly more complex.

I think it is useful to divide empires into two categories: initial empires, and those which hark back to or derive their sanctions from earlier empires. We might call these latter "secondary empires." Using these designations we can see that the Mexican empire was clearly a secondary empire while the Inca empire is, less clearly, an initial empire.

We know from archaeology that previous to the Inca empire there existed in Peru a horizon style in art that points to the existence of an impressive and unified world-view which one is tempted to assign to some kind of an empire. We know this hypothetical empire as that of Tiahuanacu (or Huari). However, we have no textual evidence whatsoever supporting the theory that Tahuantinsuyo looked back to this supposed empire as its great prototype, or indeed whether it even knew much about it. In contrast to this is the inordinate interest shown by the Mexica in the predecessor Toltec empire centered in the city of Tula; they even rested their claims to legitimacy upon their direct descent from it. This is a real dissimilarity and one which—if it should be established as true —must prove to be an exceptional tool for us to use in any analysis of late pre-Columbian empires.

Logically we should suppose that the empire which was more unified and solidly sanctioned would be that one that looked back to an imperial precedent and thus would be, in our terminology, a secondary empire. But the reverse here happens to be true. The Mexican empire —diffuse, undefined, and inefficient—was the one which looked back to a halcyon Toltec empire as a template upon which to fashion itself. Tahuantinsuyo, sophisticated in all its accounting and archival techniques, appears to have appealed to no anterior culture but solely to the pristine command of the sun god. Why this illogic?

I believe it is possible to give a fairly satisfactory answer to this question.

The Toltec empire which stood behind the first appearance of the Aztec people had been fashioned out of unusual elements. While it cast out groups as far as Yucatán and the highlands of Guatemala, this expansiveness was apparently not spearheaded by an army doing the work of the state, but was in the hands of autonomous warrior lodges or orders, particularly the Eagles and the Jaguars. It was these social institutions that the Aztecs, and particularly the Mexica, inherited out of the Toltec past and to which they ascribed superlative value. Thus it was foreordained that the Mexican state would never have an army such as Tahuantinsuyo had, namely, a cutting instrument of the state, but rather a conglomerate of warrior sodalities each with its own special cult orientation. As a setter of policy the state therefore had to compete with these discrete bodies of war-practitioners who found themselves placed strategically in the very center of the society. This entailed a constant vacillation on the part of the state as it uncertainly pursued ends which were sometimes self-interested, sometimes quixotically knightly, and occasionally imperial. No concerted and predictable policy therefore drove the Mexican state and, as a consequence, it moved erratically. And all this in spite of a prestigious derivation from the past which should have spelled stability.

Take now the contrasting case of Tahuantinsuyo. Its armies were patterned differently, being directly under the emperor's thumb. They reacted instantly to his dictates and, in effect, were extensions of him. The power structure in these armies was manifest in a professional officer class. These were not individual knights grouped in autonomous military orders.

The Inca army was thus a body responsive to the emperor. The corollary to this is that the ruler *was* the state. This situation was fully defined under Pachacuti. In brief, the continuity and relative stability of Cuzco was owing to the presence of a hero of overriding and charismatic proportions who arose at a crucial juncture. Pachacuti's influence created the milieu of power for his son and grandson, and there was no consequent need for the state to draw on the prestige and glory of an empire in the past. Here the hero in history exercised a truly overriding influence. Mexico forms a rich and complex contrast—there was not one but a multitude of heroes.

However, in our analysis of Tahuantinsuyo we must not

press our case too far, for the evidence is mainly negative. We know only that the Incas appealed to no specific empire in the past as being parental to them. The nearest they ever came to an overt acknowledgment of outside support was when they selected an alien god to exercise imperial authority in heaven.

(2)

I have often mused on the first appearance of empires and debated with myself whether empires can come into being without religious strife as a premonitory symptom. Certainly, theological turmoil attended the birth of Tahuantinsuyo. The same is not at all certain in the case of Mexico.

The Mexica were the latest of the Aztecs; they entered Anahuac as the last of the tribes and they were even then a mongrel group. Their early pantheon comprised a terrible earth-goddess (Cihuacoatl), a tribal god of portents (Huitzilopochtli), and a multitude of other deities and divine footpads. As time went on and conquest progressed, the Mexica collected a crowded roster of the most imposing Mesoamerican deities: Quetzalcoatl, Tlaloc, Xipe, Tezcatlipoca, Chalchiuhtlicue, Tlazolteotl, and others. As far as we know there were no clashes between these two sets of gods, the old and the new. Huitzilopochtli shared the high temple pyramid in Mexico with Tlaloc, a god out of the pre-Toltec times, and as the spirit of the Mexican people, Huitzilopochtli easily melded with Tonatiuh the Sun, Paynal the Runner, and a god called the Blue Sky. The ease with which these accommodations were made was one of the marks of Aztec society, itself an agglomeration.

But the gods lived in peace with each other in Mexico. One might have suspected some hostility, for instance, between the priesthood of Huitzilopochtli and that of Earth-mother Cihuacoatl; yet no one ever appeared to think that the Mexican parochial spirit, represented by Huitzilopochtli, was menaced by the universality of the great Mother, represented by Coatlicue or any other of the earth-goddesses. We know in fact of no such confrontations. Again, Huitzilopochtli could easily have run afoul of Quetzalcoatl, an absorptive and ancient god who had with great success wormed his way into Aztec thought. Such was not the case. The greater gods all lived more or less amicably side by side. Even the achievement in Aztec theology of an abstract and all-inclusive god such as Tloque Nahuaque, the *reductio* of all godhead, apparently did not wither the power or challenge the sway of Huitzilopochtli.

Thus the first appearance of empire at the time of the Tepaneca war and the severe demands it made upon the state for rethinking much of the basis of collective life, did not measurably affect the Mexica. At least it did not force them to examine the fundamentals of their constitution —and I am here assuming that fundamentals always point straight to established religious symbols and test their validity.

Herein we find notable divergence from the Inca experience. Under Viracocha Inca we are given to understand that a new god (and one more universal than Inti) stepped impulsively into Inca history to explain and sanction the new empire. Violent repercussions were at once felt when several of the Inca ayllus protested this demotion of Inti, their old tribal talisman. Proscriptions followed and while Viracocha Inca, that earthly leader of the imperial forces who took his name from the new god,

was able to promulgate the cult of the deity, the other
Inca families refused to accede.

This standoff and irresolution led directly to the weakness in the Inca state which hastened the Chanca attack.
The tribal talisman Inti, the soul of the people and the
sum of their historical experience, stood opposed to the
universalizing dogmas of such an alien creator god as
Viracocha. This creeping corrosion led to the initial
collapse of Cuzco as the Chancas broke through the Incas'
protective cordon in the Anta Basin and temporarily
defeated the god Viracocha who now retired from the
scene in the person of his deputy, the emperor Viracocha
Inca.

The sequel is instructive. The flight and defection of the
emperor Viracocha Inca allowed that singular man Pachacuti to appear as the savior of Cuzco. Which side of the
Inti-Viracocha dispute he stood on as of that moment we
do not know. There is some reason to believe that he
fudged on the issue or at least attempted to obscure it, for
he did not clearly identify that god who appeared to him
promising dominion and victory in the critical phase of
the battle. Our texts sometimes talk about this famous
apotheosis as if it were Inti appearing to his own chosen
people in the role of a savior; in other texts he appears to
be a sublime Viracocha offering the rule of the world to
Pachacuti, an offer which on any showing must have been
interpreted by the Incas as dangerous to their exclu-
siveness and prerogatives.

After some years, and only when he had shored up his
power sufficiently, did Pachacuti feel able to resolve the
ambiguity—and along with this to redesign the pattern of
subsequent Inca history in accordance with the needs of
empire. He convoked a synod in Cuzco to give a dogmatic
pronouncement on the relationships and prerogatives of

the two opposing gods. This synod proclaimed Viracocha to be the supreme god and Inti his necessary legate—a clearcut decision and one wholly in accord with the rational course of Inca history.

The needs of empire among the Incas necessarily demanded an end to ambiguity in the heavens. The principle of universal sovereignty in the heavens had to be authoritatively expounded in order to subordinate the various Inca ayllus to the new imperial (as against tribal) policy.

Among the Mexica, empire never defined itself clearly enough to create the need for a single god to supervise and sanction it. Consequently the tribal god Huitzilopochtli received no direct challenge. Even in the parlous days of the Tepaneca attack no overgod or cosmic master, incontestably sovereign, ever appeared to the Mexica leaders with oracles of hegemony. This is just another way of saying that the concept of empire was inchoate and unclear to the Mexica; not seeing it as a supreme commitment of the state, they of course envisioned no divine sanction for it.

(3)

Peace was an aim of the Inca empire, even though it was in no sense a characteristic. I am perhaps not too far wrong in using the term "Pax Incaica" here whereas the corresponding term "Pax Mexicana" would be an absurdity.

The last thing in the world the Mexica wanted was peace. Were peace to become an actuality, battles would cease and the gods whose prime nourishment was blood and hearts would starve. Thus the Mexica almost consciously goaded their imperial subjects to a breaking point and were not sorry to have to cope with the insurrections which so inevitably followed. The Inca intent, on the contrary, was the maintenance of peace within the confines of Tahuantinsuyo while war as an instrument of expansion raged outward from its boundaries. Yet the Mexica were not ignorant of what peace should be, for they had a word for it based on the adverb *tlamatca* ("peacefully, prudently, tranquilly, in repose"). It was simply that the application of the word to the condition of the empire had for them no validity.

In spite of the divergences in their concepts of imperial harmony, the two cultures agreed remarkably on one of the conditions of peace—that is, on the necessity of impounding the gods of the conquered people. It was obvious to both empires that in the gods of a conquered people was to be found the very distillation of hostility. Therefore, newly subjected groups were required to deliver up their idols as hostages, at least until such time as they had proved their loyalty. Accompanied by a skeleton priesthood and the minimum of cult appurtenances, they were escorted to Mexico or Cuzco, as the case might be, and incarcerated pending the time when they had learned subservience.

The Mexica had the most deliberate way of handling these divine prisoners. In a certain specially designed sanctuary, there were many cells and niches and, in some cases, wooden cages where these gods were installed. They were treated in other words as an entourage of slaves considered to be dangerous. In periods when the Mexican state was celebrating a festival or during a time of supplication these deities were fed on the surplus blood of the sacrifices and by that means kept alive though in a half-starved condition. A thick pavement of encrusted blood lay under each cage. Should the province from which they came and which they represented attempt rebellion, they were dragged out, reviled and mistreated, and subjected to neglect and further starvation. In Aztec theology they corresponded to demons.

An incident in Inca history reveals a similar train of thought. The emperor Huascar had been oracularly encouraged by all the huacas of the empire to believe that, in the contest then shaping up between him and his half-brother Atauhuallpa, it would be he who would be the victor. In the battles which followed, the opposite was consistently true; with every new dispatch from the north it was learned that the enemy had again routed the imperial forces and was moving even closer to Cuzco. Huascar, finally, in desperation summoned all of the named and many of the captive gods of empire to a meeting. Standing in the center of a circle of these demonic prisoners and allies, all of them lumpy, unshapen, and silent, he rounded on them, accusing them of treachery. He ended a hysterical harangue by cursing them all as devils and deceivers. This performance well displays the connection made by the Incas between the hostility of such gods in exile and any ill luck which befell the empire. Even as prisoners such gods were able to work Tahuantinsuyo harm. In this instance they had done this, not by malfeasance, but by slyly seducing Huascar through mendacious oracles and perverted omens of success.

(4)

We have mentioned Topa Inca's seizure of the distant shrine of Titicaca and his forced integration of this cult into the imperial religion. Even more important for an analysis of Tahuantinsuyo was his seizure of the mythology of this sacred island. It speaks of a high order of statecraft that the imperial house so lucidly realized the need of a cosmic mythology to fit its mission, and that it fixed on one so appropriate. This mythology will be described in the next chapter so it is unnecessary to outline it here. What is of moment is to note the circumstances under which this came to pass.

Viracocha Inca had discovered a foreign god (Viracocha) more lordly than Inti, as we have already learned —one with glorious achievements and jurisdiction over the whole of creation. Inti's interests were confined to matters in which the Inca ayllus alone participated. Pachacuti, the son of Viracocha Inca, had in synod declared that the new god theologically outranked Inti and thus was that deity who alone could patronize the empire. But this was still only dogma and lacked the compelling power of a mythological event and a locus. Topa Inca would provide this and thus complete the conceptual evolution of Tahuantinsuyo's place in the universe.

The ruins of Tiahuanacu on the southern shores of the great lake called by us Titicaca (but which was referred to earlier as Lake Chucuito) were already some four hundred years in existence before the Incas. The tumbled blocks spoke of marvels out of the past and of a greatness no longer attainable. The lake itself was very holy and played a role in bygone events of vast significance. It was at Tiahuanacu, as a matter of fact, where the god Viracocha had first unveiled the created heavens and earth. In the southern part of the lake was that exceptionally sacred island called Titicaca, the "Rock of the Cat." Attached to this rock was the story of the first light ever to come out of the eternal darkness. A cult memorialized this pristine event. Who the originators of this cult were we do not know but when Topa Inca carried Inca arms down into those regions he ostentatiously worshipped at the great shrine and, not unexpectedly, discovered that the cosmic event which the cult harked back to had been also connected with Manco Capac's appearance and the assignment to him of dominion over the whole world.

This henceforth became dogma and cogently supported Inca claims to total prerogative. Without such a sacred tale, the Incas could not have proved to strangers their legitimate right to rule the whole earth.

The same building blocks existed for the Mexica but they never finally, and for all time, fitted the keystone into the imperial arch. Near Mexico and some thousand years before its founding there had existed a great city. Just as Tiahuanacu had been long in ruins at the time of the Incas so this city also had been in ruins at the time of the entry of the Aztecs into the Valley of Mexico as in the case of Tiahuanacu, it became in the minds of later people the very place of creation and the birthplace of the first light. Those who spoke Nahuatl called it Teotihuacán, "The Place Where The God (i.e., the sun) was Created," thereby recognizing its decisive role in the history of the cosmos.

In Aztec times the site of the ruins of Teotihuacan belonged to Tezcoco, the city allied with Mexico. Mexico made no attempt either to seize the site or to splice its story of genesis onto the story of their own origins, which would thus have showed them as holders of a franchise to universal dominion. Their failure to do this is significant of the fact that they read the world differently from the Incas; to the Mexica, man was not a partner or coworker in the cosmos but a slave, despised and of lowly origin, his task to be no more than a butler to the gods. The

Mexican could not take in the possibility of a surrogate mastery over the whole world. He did not really believe that he was only a little lower than the angels.

(5)

Empire perforce creates a terminology. We have already referred to the Inca empire as Tahuantinsuyo, the Four Quarters. By this the Incas meant the whole world, which concept in turn implied that there could be only one of its kind, in other words, only one empire. Nevertheless the word Tahuantinsuyo does not mean "empire"—nor is there such a term in Quechua. There is only a word for "realm" (*capaccay*) which has to be further modified to give even an approximation of our "empire."

The Aztec empire—or, more accurately, the three mingled empires of Mexico, Tezcoco, and Tlacopan—had no geographic name for itself comparable to Tahuantinsuyo unless we consider *Cemanahuac* as filling the bill. Cemanahuac means "the whole of the land between the waters," the waters referred to here being the Pacific Ocean and the Gulf of Mexico. Another approximation might be the phrase meaning "great city" or "state," *huei altepetl,* which is perfectly matched in Quechua by *capac llacta* also translated as "great city." But though both of these terms can refer to states or nations, we are wrong to assume that they also mean "empire." For this purpose they are inexact because they keep the concept tied to the city-state at the center of empire. Our word for empire is based on the Latin *imperium* which carries the concept of command and centers therefore on control rather than on geography.

Rather than attempting to identify a specific word for empire we should rather seek a word for "emperor." Here we find evidence for our previously expressed belief that while Tahuantinsuyo was a true empire, the Mexica empire was unfixed and lacked definition. The emperor in Cuzco was the *sapay capac Inca*, "the only Royal Inca" and he is thus stated to be unique whereas the emperor in Mexico was the *huei tlatoani*, "the great ruler," a term which could also be applied to his equally great ally, the tlatoani of Tezcoco. The Nahuatl term is not exclusive as is the Inca one. We may conjecture therefore that only the Quechua phrase conceptually approaches our own word for "emperor."

There is an additional scrap of information supporting this. The sapay capac Inca was what he was because of his absolute purity of blood and this was gained by the fact that he was married to his full sister thus producing absolutely legitimate offspring. There is no such obligatory royal incest in the Aztec picture which fact again is in line with our contention that the Mexica had no clear definition of the concept of an emperor.

(6)

We have been led to the conclusion that the divergences between the Inca and the Aztec worlds can be grasped by noting the presence of the imperial concept in one and the near absence of it in the other. We have also analyzed the Mexican case and found that one of the reasons—and probably the most important one—for this failure to attain a unitary concept was the teuctli's divided loyalty. This personage not only fought for the state in its endeavors to establish a wider sphere of influence and power, he also fought that he might die splendidly and serve the appetitive needs of the gods. The Incas yoked their fighting men more tightly to the interests of the state. Successful empire demands thoroughly obedient and otherwise uncommitted warriors and bureaucrats. This is because the policies and objectives of the imperialistic state are excessively demanding and do not abide other faiths.

Perhaps I can summarize all this.

The Mexica did not attain to empire in the full sense. The Mexican warrior, by displaying noteworthy valor, could be promoted up into one of the great knightly orders that fought wars as a rite and not primarily in response to orders from the state. Mexico was a compromise between the self-interested and sovereign demands of a city-state on the one hand, and on the other the self-sacrificing commitment of her chief warriors to a purpose beyond the state. Tahuantinsuyo, on the contrary, claimed to have found its structures outlined on the very blueprint of creation itself. Its commands were by delegation the commands of heaven and were thereby unimpeachable.

7

The Divine Presence

(1)

Much as we might be tempted, we cannot really say that the Inca state was more secular than the Mexican state. From everything that I have written up to now this would seem to be a necessary deduction. Not so. The Incas were every bit as aware of and responsive to the supernatural as were the Mexica. It was in the cultural organization of this responsiveness that the two differed so widely.

Here we must consider briefly the two words *huaca* and *teotl* from the Quechua and Nahuatl languages, respectively. Both roughly correspond to our "godhead," "divinity," of "the divine."

Huaca signifies primarily the holiness that is in a place, a person, a demon, a god, or any unusual object. A god could have huaca only insofar as he had about him the obviously odd, the miraculous, or the efficient. This is just such an immediate feeling for the sacred as we expect to find at a Neolithic level of society. The corresponding Nahuatl word is less obvious. *Teotl* is applied specifically to the sun (when his name Tonatiuh is not mentioned) as if he were *the* "god" par excellence. The gods grouped

together are always referred to as *teteo* (plural) and we
have thus a fairly exact equivalent of our own "god" or
"gods."

Huaca and teotl are thus not fully synonymous. The
first one points to the divine under manifold aspects of
power and otherness; the second narrowly identifies that
power as being anthropomorphic. We would expect to
find them reversed—especially in view of the fact that the
Incas could conceive of omnipotence in Viracocha,
whereas there was really no such solitary and outstanding
figure in the Aztec pantheon.

Viracocha was a high god, sublime, nomistic, and
mythic. Other gods, other demons, and a plentiful repository of huaca existed outside of and beside him, but he
held true empire over them all for he had created them
all. Having no mate and no palpable form he was
conceived of in the more exalted levels of speculation as
sheer authority. Possessing also a specific locale as far as
his creative powers went, a place where he had called into
being all the varieties of human culture, he was also a
person. Therefore by definition he was a true god. The
Incas felt no need to narrow the meaning of huaca to
include and describe him, for the name Viracocha was the
equivalent of our "Lord" as it refers to the Creator of all
things. This means that the Incas did indeed have a word
for "God" but that the word for it was *viracocha;* and this
word was even more narrowly conceived than was teotl
for it could only mean "that god who was Viracocha or
was like Viracocha or who represented his will." The
Aztecs also had the concept of a high god (Tloque
Nahuaque for instance, or Ipalnemoani) but he was a
philosophical abstraction considered to be a teotl and
assigned as an alter ego to the trickster god Tezcatlipoca.

In brief, the Aztec world of the supernatural was

pluralistic—all beings in it, all powers, were teotl. The Inca world of the supernatural comprised two levels, the powers or "huaca" and above that Viracocha, lord of all huacas. Again we find that the picture of the heavens portrayed by these two cultures fits well into our thesis that one of the cultures was a novice, the other a comparative sophisticate, in empire.

(2)

Yet when we superficially compare the two pantheons they look remarkably similar.

Both nations had high gods. The Incas saw Viracocha as a true god and a spirit. The Aztecs saw Tloque Nahuaque as partially that but more generally they saw him as a philosophical principle, a ground of being. No myths attach to the latter's name, but he was invoked under many captions. He is Ipalnemoani, "he by virtue of whom we live," an epithetical god presuming almost all of the other prominent gods of the Aztec cosmos; he is also "the Inventor of Himself" and "the Invisible One." Mixcoatl, Tezcatlipoca, Huitzilopochtli, and Tonatiuh can all be said to be him, i.e., to be avatars of him. Among the Incas no god could be an avatar of Viracocha.

As Tloque Nahuaque he was "the Abeyant One." The attempt here is to express philosophically the essences of the gods and then to further refine this distillation into a new god—the process seems, however, not to have been completely achieved, for Tloque Nahuaque was never said to rule over the other gods. In other words the Aztecs, lacking the full imperial concept, were consequently unable to apply it to the concept of the high god; no one god was incontestably at the summit of authority and judgment.

Tloque Nahuaque thus remained in the realm of thought. He was an embellishment on the concept of teotl, not a modification of it. In the case of the Incas the empire could not have been maintained without the concept of Viracocha as a spiritual person, supreme and universal. He was thus a true god and not a mere abstraction. The two pantheons also form a contrast. The Inca pantheon is comparatively homogeneous and seems to be indigenous. Inti (who becomes the sun) possesses a consort, Mama Quilla, the Moon. Their court is served by the stellar and atmospheric hosts as pages, the Rainbow, the Pleiades, Venus, and others. Illapa the Storm God who wields the thunderbolt and brings the rain is paired with the earth mother in a primitive agricultural dyad. On another level, however, the earth mother appears as *sui generis,* without connections and without impediments. She appears under several names and with many powers which seem, on the level of the thoroughly primitive, to be the equivalents of the powers exercised by Viracocha over the cosmic state.

Anomalies, however, existed. The deity Huanacauri, giver of victory in war, had to be kept outside of Cuzco on his mountain top some fifteen miles away. Here he had been found in the early Inca past and here he had insisted on remaining, to the detriment of Inca logic. We can thus see a certain amount of accumulation behind the standard Inca pantheon. The gods do not form a compact body of Olympians melded into an extended family under a patriarch; they are grouped into at least three categories or clusters, with only that one centering about Inti as the image of the state.

The Mexican pantheon is better described as a *pot pourri,* a jumble of gods, many of them vaguely related to each other but in a way that defies precise analysis. There

was the sun-god Tonatiuh but he was without relationship
to Metztli the Moon, who in any case was of minor
importance. The planet Venus was powerful and ominous
and intimately involved in the cult of sacrifice. The
storm-god Tlaloc was given the honor in cult of sitting
beside the patron god of the Mexica Huitzilopochtli yet
there is absolutely no connection between them. Occasionally Tlaloc is said to be married to a goddess of
waters, Chalchiuhtlicue. Quetzalcoatl, Mictlanteuctli,
Yopi, Tezcatlipoca, Tlazolteotl, all of them massive and
important deities were simply listed in enumerations with
no principle of relatedness to bind them together into
any kind of constitution except when they temporarily
usurped the masks and jurisdictions of others.

Mother earth appeared here, as she did to the Incas, in
many forms but always recognizable as the giver and
destroyer of life and as the supreme oracle. She was
conceived of as a thing of horror and was both eternal and
demonic. Whereas the Incas felt her power as a vast
slumbrous huaca encysting the whole life of a people, a
kind of suspiring matrix of rock and soil, the Mexica saw
her as a demonic colossus gaping and clashing her skeletal
jaws. It was a difference not in any essential quality but in
the degree of hostility which she showed toward men who
lived in her bosom.

The Mexican pantheon was highly eclectic and included her major gods from many other lands. This
comports with the pluralistic view of the supernatural
which the Mexica possessed. To them the cosmos was a
variegated and four-sided realm wherein the gods jostled
against each other, adding color and a fierce drama to the
understanding of life but also preventing men from
realizing the possibilities of direction in history. The
Mexica knew the lot of men to be contemptible and mean.

The gods were creatures of whim, beings of great power not concerned with responsibilities and not forced by any law of their natures to take a stand for or against mankind. The Mexican world of the supernatural was filled with heroic or nightmare beings striding restlessly hither and yon as if among flames.

The crueler upland earth of Peru seems to have fostered among its people a somewhat more reliable set of gods and goddesses, beings who could be depended on in general to perform their tasks for the good of the state, if not for the good of the individual.

(3)

The parts which the sun played in Mexico and in Cuzco again form a contrast of near opposites.

The Inca sun was Punchao, a word which is equally well translated as "day" though basically it referred to the disc of the sun. Almost exactly synonymous was Tonatiuh, the Aztec sun-disc. But on top of these common and similar understandings of the shining orb itself, there were foisted in each case widely contrasting secondary interpretations.

The Incas early took Punchao and fused him with their tribal mascot Inti; soon Inti became the common designation for the sun as a god, and not merely the physical face of the sun. From this it followed that inasmuch as Inti was the father of all Incas so they were the very children of the sun. The Mexica correspondingly took Tonatiuh and fused him with Huitzilopochtli, their tribal mascot, but with the difference that the fusion was incomplete. While Huitzilopochtli was the god of all the Mexica as the sun he remained the special god of the Eagle knights. Thus the identification was not close enough to turn the Mexica as a people incontestably into kinsmen of the sun. And in fact even the Eagle knights saw him not as their distinguished progenitor but solely as the model of the perfect warrior. The precision of the Inca concept tying Inti to the sun and the Incas to Inti as their father is thus in marked contrast to the confusion and richness of the corresponding Mexican symbols.

Had Mexico succeeded in metamorphosing Tonatiuh into Huitzilopochtli it would have meant that the knightly orders would no longer have been able to play an autonomous role, but would thenceforth have been reduced to a corps of armed men under the control of the state. This, of course, did not happen.

(4)

But what about the concept of evil and its recognition by the Aztecs and Incas? All peoples linked in communities as articulated as these two are fully able to distinguish the principle of erosion and hostility which afflicts them socially. The identification of this principle is a theological crux in any study of a society and reveals its most fundamental beliefs.

The Incas believed in Supay, generally thought to have been a perverse son of Viracocha but still a being permanently at home in the universe. His delight was in destruction, revolution, deceit, and sudden surprises. He possessed a huaca which—in theory, lesser than Viracocha's huaca—nevertheless was in practice known to be eternal. His name can be with some accuracy translated as the "shadow." He was phantasmal and found everywhere in Peru, not just among the Incas.

One can almost say that, if Supay had not already existed, Tahuantinsuyo would have been obliged to create him, so necessary to a great empire is the objectification of the forces that menace its precarious stability. If Viracocha was the palladium of the Inca empire, Supay was the guilty recognition that the empire was indeed maintained by a most monstrous tyranny.

Supay had a cult and there were certain shamans who served him when they became possessed by his spirit. As was said above, this cult of the malfeasant god was spread throughout Peru and was not limited to the Incas alone. They, however, expanded his domain and cast him in a large and honorable role as Viracocha's adversary. His mythology is much to the point in trying to understand the realism that underlay Tahuantinsuyo. When Viracocha anciently was engaged in the act of creation, he was accompanied by three sons, one of whom was named Tawapaca; this son possessed his father's huaca but inverted it for he became rebellious and went about altering the grand works of his father, twisting them, crippling them, and diluting their pristine quality. This duplicity accounts for all the disharmony in the world. Viracocha ordered his two obedient sons to bind the evil one and cast him adrift on Lake Titicaca. Cursing and threatening vengeance, Supay (for this is who Tawapaca was) drifted away to the south. Some say he returned with the claim that he was his father, but in any case all men know that he still lives and is the author of all deceits.

There is nothing at all comparable to this in Aztec myth. No god stars in the role of the devil. It is true that a god like Tezcatlipoca tricks the wise and benign Quetzalcoatl and is known to suddenly reverse the good fortune of men and rulers, but this is always from a whim and not from an established bent in his nature. Often, indeed,

Tezcatlipoca does the opposite, raising men up to wealth and honor as it momentarily pleases him. He is dangerous and pitiless but he is not perforce and always evil.

It is quite evident that the Mexica arrived at no understanding of total malice in history, of the spirit of unmaking, for they had no concept of its opposite, namely a Creator in whose being was contained the law of all rightness, one who in fact maintained an appointed empire on earth displaying this rightness. Needless to say the Mexica understood evil as well as did the Incas, of this there can be no doubt, but they believed that it belonged to godhead as a principle in exactly the same sense as did goodness. Thus they felt no need to oppose the two qualities—which to us seem so contradictory—allotting one to the Creator and maintainer and the other to his antagonist, a deceiver and destroyer. The Incas believed evil to be unprincipled and directed against their achievements. Therefore they knew Supay to be an adversary.

(5)

Another outstanding similarity between the two cultures is to be found in their understanding of time. Both of them believed in the aeonic and catastrophic nature of time, but the Aztecs carried this belief to a most dramatic extreme.

The Aztecs identified the aeon in which we are now living as the fifth one to have existed; the Incas appear to have come to the same conclusion but not with the same hard clarity. For the Mexica this present aeon came into being when the gods gathered in the ruins of Teotihuacán and called up out of the darkness the sun and the moon. It was only after this magnificent illumination that men were created. The aeon was broken up into lustrums each comprised of fifty-two years. At the conclusion of one of these units the aeon itself would end in a general collapse and a return to primeval darkness, the destruction being wrought by earthquakes shaking all things to bits.

Within this general Aztec concept (but not jarring with it) was a variant that was specifically Mexican and which involved the return of the man-god Quetzalcoatl. Here the cosmos was equated specifically with the Mexican realm while the whole of aeonic time was equated with the period beginning with the Toltec domination, it being the settled belief of the Mexica that they themselves were neo-Toltecs and therefore legitimately carrying on the earlier great empire. The sacred ruler of the Toltecs, Quetzalcoatl, had been ousted from his seat of rule in Tula and after many vicissitudes had disappeared eastward into the Gulf of Mexico. Beyond those waters he settled in a distant home, generally identified with Yucatán, awaiting there the day when he would return to reclaim his lost patrimony. This patrimony, the empire, was being held in trust against his return by the Mexican royal house. It was obvious that that dread return would end the present era by unseating the Mexican royalty.

There are also references in our Peruvian sources to earlier aeons, where the past aeons were destroyed by the creator in disgust at certain inept creatures whom he had at the time formed. The aeon preceding the present one is said to have been destroyed by a universal deluge. Whereas most of the Peruvian peoples believed that a favored couple escaped the great flood by climbing a high mountain and living to repopulate the new aeon, the Incas believed that all things were at that time destroyed and reverted to chaos. Out of this blackness and standing on his rock of Titicaca, as has already been related, Viracocha called forth the sun and then the Inca people, entrusting to them their divine mission. The various tribes of men he molded out of clay. Then he left Tiahuanacu and moved slowly northward up the spine of Peru designating territories for the various tribes, identifying their varied garb and manner of speaking, and teaching them the arts of agriculture, llama-herding, and house-building. Having thus culturally arranged the whole world and arriving on the Ecuadorian coast, he then sailed away and disappeared out of the sight of men. But he indicated before he left that he would some day return and close the aeon. That such a day would spell finis for Tahuantinsuyo was obvious to the Incas.

Thus both peoples believed in the periodicity of creation and in the special precariousness of this one which was to end with the return of the god. Specifically this return would unseat the great emperors of the earth, both Aztec and Inca. It was the closest that either culture ever got to the idea of nemesis.

The Aztec picture of time was carefully and anxiously elaborated whereas the corresponding Inca picture lacked vividness. In the latter, knowledge about the exact number of aeons in the past was not really a matter of interest. Over each of the five Mexican aeons a different god ruled whereas in the corresponding Inca myth there was only one creator which smudged considerably the belief in multiple creations; nor does one become aware in Inca lore of the same great pulse of creations, each one sharply differentiated from all preceding ones as in the Aztec tales.

We can see that time to the Incas was not of superlative importance. They thought in terms of empire rather than in temporal terms. Tahuantinsuyo—so inclusive, so ubiquitous, so colossal that its existence was perforce the

measure of all things—this was the important considera-
tion, not the mere enumeration of years. For the Incas
time stood aside while their institutions fulfilled their
functions. That very abeyance substituted for time and its
passage. Thus there was no overriding insistence on the
ephemera of existence. In their gigantic efforts to erect and
maintain a sacred empire, the Incas were dulled to the
spiritual concerns of individual men—in any case always
seen as petty by bureaucratic eyes.

The Mexica felt time to be a presence at once myste-
rious and hostile, and far more real in its effects than
anything men could create. Time could be endlessly
probed by men, and indeed was so probed and explored,
but its dangers were not thereby lessened. It was so
overpowering that it absorbed the thoughts of the Aztecs,
made them feel like wraiths caught up briefly in a fog of
lies and appearances and then blown out like lights in the
night. Above all it made them aware of their mortality.
The warrior fought to achieve death for he found no way
of linking time with the robustness of life. Time was a
slayer.

(6)

One further investigation in this vein must detain us:
the meaning behind the Quechua *huaoqui* and the Nahuatl
nahualli. Both words are attempts to elucidate the relationship of an individual to the supernatural world. They are
spiritual concepts and of importance in our search for
likes and unlikes.

Huaoqui in Quechua primarily means "brother" or
"friend." The Incas believed that they each possessed a
huaoqui, indeed without it the fullness of human experi-

ence could not be attained. A huaoqui was an extruded self which was contained in some object, generally an image or fetish. Commoners were not thought to possess them.

The huaoqui seems at first to have been restricted to members of the royal line and only later to have been taken up by Incas of collateral and noble lines. The identification of one's huaoqui and the naming of it was a conscious and ceremonial act. Once identified, a huaoqui shared in a person's vitality and in particular became almost one with his luck or fortune. It was interested in his welfare, it accompanied him to war or received veneration in his absence, informed him of intrigues and ambushes, and offered him oracular advice. When the huaoqui selected happened also to be the statue of a god it obviously could exert massive powers. Pachacuti, for instance, chose as his huaoqui an image of the god of the thunderbolt, Chuqui Illa.

An Inca's death in no sense altered the powers of his huaoqui, which continued to serve and to extend his existence. Even gods (considered as individuals) possessed their own huaoquis. Thus a huaoqui was antithetically both a person's extracorporeal self and an annexed power. It is probably best thought of as an amalgam of soul and patron saint.

The *nahualli* of an Aztec, on the contrary, was inherited from an ancestor or was assigned to him at birth by a priest. The word is instructive for it most probably comes from an old verb meaning "to deceive, dissemble, muffle up, or disguise." Generally the nahualli was an animal double which was a detached alter ego, living its own life but indissolubly linked with the living person. No one could say for certain whether the man or his animal double was primary for either could shift shape and take on the aspects of the other. The wounding or death of one was automatically and instantaneously the wounding or death of the other; though they were two disjoined bodies, they shared one life. All men, whether rulers or commoners, partook democratically in this two-shape system, though not all made the same intensive uses of it. Some men's—and all gods'—personal power was such that they easily controlled both worlds, and when they shifted shapes it was generally for evil or dangerous purposes. The coyote was a nahualli of the god Tezcatlipoca and expressed the suddenness and slyness of that god. Jaguars, wolves, owls, and serpents were common beast-doubles. Men who superlatively possessed such nahuallis were feared for their enchantments and formed a notable class of sorcerers.

Thus we have on the Inca side a relatively benign and elective system restricted to an exclusive caste and affording its membership a powerful addition of spirituality. On the Mexican side we find the corresponding system to be always fateful and often sinister; all men could participate in it and it did not therefore distinguish Aztecs from other men.

8

Two Consummations

(1)

In nothing so much as in their endings did the Inca and the Mexica more resemble each other. The events attendant upon the downfall of these two cultures are so epic in scope and so similar in detail that the careful historian and the casual reader of history are equally reduced to wonder. The former is embarrassed and publicly pretends to be unable to see the identity; the latter glibly solves it with the cliché that "history repeats itself."

History does not repeat itself. Being made up of countless intertwined decisions of men great and small everywhere, each of whom is unique and many of whom are mistaken, it cannot ever repeat itself. On the contrary, it is endlessly different. The explanation is not that history repeats itself, but that all men labor in the same vineyard and have similar desires, designs, capacities for self-deception, and a common mortality. Out of such a shared destiny comes the pattern of men inventing cultures and creating workable institutions which finally become rigid and lead to decline or demise. But the specific events, the cultural matrix, and the elapsed time are so different in every case as to produce histories which are truly *sui generis*. In this concluding chapter I propose to comment at some length on this paradox as I find it applying to these two civilizations.

(2)

Let us begin with a summary of the two chronologies. We have already had occasion to note that behind each of the two civilizations loom earlier ones which were greatly prestigious. These forerunners collapsed and were followed by poorly recorded dark periods. Then out of a deep twilight of peoples our own two appear. The Incas had advanced into the upper end of the Huatanay Valley where Cuzco was situated about A.D. 1250. The Aztecs traditionally left Coatepec, the mountain near Tula, where they had found Huitzilopochtli, and headed for Anahuac in roughly the same year. These two events are the first we can discover which define the two groups as nations and our interest in them lies in this contemporaneity. Having founded their respective capitals, both peoples then suffered sustained attacks. From these crises they emerged as renewed and thenceforth imperial peoples; this happened to the Mexica in the year 1428, and to the Incas in 1438, ten years later. From that point on foreign adventures became characteristic of both histories.

The critical point in the careers of the mature empires —and the coincidences which concern us here—begin with the first appearance of internal dissension. With the death of the famous Nezahualpilli of Tezcoco in 1515 (eight years before the end), Mexico actively began the dismantling of the Three City League which up to that time had been its strongest support. Huayna Capac probably died in the year 1525 (eight years before the end) leaving the empire hopelessly split between his two sons. In 1519 the Spaniards landed on the Gulf coast of Mexico and two years later conquered Tenochtitlan. In 1531 the Spanish arrived in Peru and in two years had seized Cuzco and destroyed Tahuantinsuyo.

This is all very spectacular and is certainly not without meaning. But let us now look more closely into those events.

(3)

In the year 1499 the Aztec empire was at its height. Ahuitzotl stretched out his hand far to the southeast in search of the rich cacao lands on the Pacific slopes of Guatemala, a region to which no Aztec ruler had penetrated before. In the year 1511, called by rebellion in the north, Huayna Capac went up into Ecuador taking his court with him, an exercise of sublime insouciance inasmuch as it left the sacred city of Cuzco unattended by majesty. Tahuantinsuyo was then at its most splendid. Both of these moves would commit their respective states to new adventures. Such grandiose actions are quite what we would expect of empires in their *floruit*.

It was not long after these events that certain wispy rumors which had been floating disconnectedly about in Central America and down the shores of the Pacific suddenly took on frightening proportions. In 1510 a terrible pillar of light was visible throughout Mesoamerica, appearing each day in the east before dawn and lasting almost a full year. The Aztecs shuddered. In 1522 Huayna Capac was receiving reports of untoward events in the far north, of strange beings fishing for pearls and sweeping the seas in vessels like temples.

Scraps of information continued to float in from such transoceanic sources, the more terrible for being garbled. Then probably in 1526 Huayna Capac died of a virulent disease that had been introduced into Tahuantinsuyo by the Spaniards but which preceded by several years their actual presence there. It was whispered that impure and stunted apparitions had come to the emperor prophesying his death and then had vanished without trace. In 1515, as we have mentioned, Nezahualpilli of Tezcoco died; he was the greatest figure among all the contemporary Aztecs, a famous seer, and he had earlier predicted a coming doom for the whole of the Aztec world—a doom associated with invaders. These two deaths left gaps in both worlds and set in train the disorders to come.

In 1517 the first important Spanish explorer out of Cuba, Francisco Hernández de Córdoba, appeared off Yucatán. This fact was soon known by the Aztecs many hundreds of miles away. In 1527 Pizarro, on his second voyage, was standing off the coast of Peru, which fact, too, was promptly reported in Tahuantinsuyo. In both cases rumors now were more solidly founded but no less frightening for being more circumstantial. In the case of the Mexica, the new beings were thought to be the sons of Quetzalcoatl coasting back as had been so often predicted; in the case of the Incas they were thought to be *viracochas*, harbingers of the creator announcing his return.

In the year 1528 the foundations of the war that racked Tahuantinsuyo were laid when Atauhuallpa gave up his efforts to conciliate his brother Huascar, the legitimate emperor, and prepared for the inevitable contest. In 1516 Mexico broke up the Three City League and set out to thoroughly dominate it. Thus threatened, Tezcoco split into factions and an army of refugees fled north to prepare for war with Mexico.

In 1519 Cortés landed and arrested Moteuczoma. In 1532 Pizarro appeared in Peru and in the same year captured Atauhuallpa, who had just been informed of his victory over Huascar and was therefore the acknowledged emperor of Tahuantinsuyo. In 1520 Moteuczoma was killed, undoubtedly by his Spanish captors. In 1533 Pizarro executed the captive Atauhuallpa.

Finally in the year 1521 the city of Mexico capitulated to the Spaniards and was destroyed, having first ruptured internally, shedding bitter fraternal blood. In 1533 Cuzco was forced open and taken by the Spaniards. Both seizures were accompanied by the installation of puppet emperors under Spanish direction.

What is of interest in this list is not only the basic resemblance of the events but the uncanny similarity in their tempo. Inca history followed corresponding Aztec developments by from ten to thirteen years, no more, no less. This strange regularity in the sequence of events cannot fail to impress the historian.

(4)

The fall of empires is generally shrouded in mysteries, in hair-raising uncertainties, in momentary successes, and rhythmic collapses, or else in sudden and total disappearance. In the case of a slow and faltering demise nothing makes any one setback the climactic one, and one can always expect a hero who will appear and reverse the trend.

In the case of our two empires we can see from the above that something else is at work which gives us the feeling of the end's predictability. This "something else" is the return of the god prophesied in each case, a belief which by its mere presence premolded events into the predicted pattern. The fact that both the Aztec and the Inca worlds possessed such similar understandings of the ominous culmination of time meant that both insensibly moved in such ways as to bring about events which to us appear the same.

The Toltec priest-king Quetzalcoatl was known by his birthdate name, One-Reed. It had become a part of the myth of his return that he would reappear in the year One-Reed which according to the cycle could come up only once every fifty-two years. It happened by coincidence that the year of Cortés's landing, which was 1519 in the Gregorian calendar, corresponded to the year One-Reed in the Mexican calendar. That which we explain as coincidence the Mexica saw as the inevitable fulfillment of the signs of the past, a monstrous birth from a delayed and awful pregnancy. It was this which produced the succeeding paralysis of the Mexican state.

The dreadfulness of the coincidence had been preceded by a long series of bodings and misadventures going back at least fourteen years before the landing. In the year 1505 a drought of serious proportions afflicted the Aztec states in the Valley of Mexico. Then had followed a series of portents, later much exaggerated by hindsight but still indicative of the mood of the times. Rumors were spurred by Spanish activities in the Caribbean: Columbus's explorations of the Honduran coast in 1499, Solís and Pinzón at Chetumal in 1506, the shipwreck among the Mayans of certain Spaniards from Panama in 1511, and other such events. Rumors based on such landfalls fed on themselves and because they found a ready matrix in the myth of the god's return, they were strengthened in that direction and adequately accounted for.

These unsettling developments received a radical imprint in Mexico reflecting the personality of Moteuczoma II. He was a man of a frightening intensity and whichever way his mind inclined so was oriented the fever of the times. Himself spiritually disturbed, he read the continuing series of rumors as if they were directed at him alone rather than at all of Mesoamerica. He fell rapidly into abjectness and despair and his loss of decisiveness finally paralyzed the whole of the state apparatus; with monstrous regularity he convoked meetings in council, always fruitless, and in the upshot hopelessly divided his magnates. Sorcerers and the custodians of holy books were also called upon, thus increasing the confusion.

We must remember that this was the situation in a world where the Mexican state, now at last the sole and supreme political power in the Aztec world, was still less than sovereign owing to the supernatural allegiance of its knights.

This indecisiveness in the Mexican picture is duplicated in Tahuantinsuyo by the uncertainties introduced into the workings of the state by Huayna Capac's irresponsible transfer of the capital from Cuzco to the remote Ecuadorian north. This occurred only a short time before rumors began to flood in from coastal merchants of strange men in the north (Panama) and of ship sightings. Huayna Capac's whole Ecuadorian campaign—the most extensive and weighty ever mounted by any Inca emperor—was an extravaganza and his death away from Cuzco turned it into a disaster, for he died leaving the empire by testament partitioned vaguely between two sons, the legitimate heir in Cuzco and the favorite in Quito. The rumors which had preceded this inopportune death were capped by the arrival of the devastating plague originating among the Panamanian Spaniards. In Peru its ravages were widespread and swift. From the year of Huayna

Capac's death on, the Peruvians, like the Mesoamericans in a similar situation, lived with rumors and lurid fancies, and became progressively more disoriented.

As Moteuczoma's personality was a factor in the disintegration of the Mexica so, too, was the impact of Huascar, Huayna Capac's son and successor, on Tahuantinsuyo. It is hard to see clearly through the Babylonian murk of that last legitimate reign, but it appears that Huascar was egregious in all his ways, disaster-prone and, in fact, almost certainly mad in a historical sense. Every decision he was to make in the affairs leading up to his war upon Atauhuallpa was wrong and entailed exactly the results one might have expected. Finally with his back to the wall he appealed to the unreliable huacas of the empire for support. Like Moteuczoma he ended up confronting those gods, but unlike Moteuczoma he found the power to curse them and drive them from the temple. Not that it did him much good.

Moteuczoma's new order, instituted at the time when he first came to power in 1503 (eighteen years before the end), was as little able to provide stability in the crisis of the Spanish invasion as was Huayna Capac's abandonment of Cuzco to absentee rule in 1511 (twenty-two years before the end).

(5)

The ends of these empires were both preceded by intestine war, a development not unexpected. A civil war is easily distinguished from the broils which often accompany the setting up of a state. Civil war is a sign that the fully formed state is beginning to swing erratically in its search for a policy. The violence that marks it is the sign that no policy can be willingly accepted.

There had been admonitory upheavals in the state following the splendid reigns of Topa Inca and Moteuczoma I. In the first case it had been the mutiny of the Lower Cuzco regiment while Huayna Capac was on his Ecuadorian campaign. This deep rift was patched over somewhat superficially. In the case of Mexico the split between the two moieties came in 1473, the year when Tlatilulco attacked Tenochtitlan and was itself almost destroyed in the process. These seismic shakings of our two states occurred well before rumors of the gods' return had appeared. When the Spaniards did intrude, the convulsions thereby induced in the state found the weakened joint in the constitution and finally forced the two halves permanently apart.

The civil war between Atauhuallpa and Huascar was most probably an attack by Lower Cuzco (represented by Atauhuallpa in the north who was free from the stringencies ordained by residence in the capital) on Upper Cuzco. Huascar in his erratic courses seems to have divorced himself from membership in Upper Cuzco, being aware of the shakiness of his own moiety's support. At any rate civil war was the result ("the War of the Two Brothers"), bitter, without quarter, and total. Atauhuallpa and the party of the north triumphed, but even before they were able to reach out and pluck the fruits of victory Pizarro had intervened. The fact that Tahuantinsuyo was still suffering the trauma of violent division reduced its ability to deal with the interlopers.

In the case of Mexico, the Three City League had been weakened by Moteuczoma II and this led in 1516, as has been shown, to the drive for total dominion. Powerful forces in Tezcoco immediately arose to contest this usurpation by Mexico. Admittedly this was not civil war within Mexico but was tantamount to it, for the Three City League had been an absolutely indispensable part of Mexican policy since its inception back in the Tepaneca war.

As regards civil war in Mexico itself, this did not break out until a few months after the deaths of Moteuczoma II and his successor Cuitlahuac. Both of these rulers had been Tenochcas. The death of the latter led to an open revulsion against the dominant Tenochca house, the proscription of some of its eminent members, and the election of Cuauhtemoc, a nobleman closely allied with the people of Tlatilulco.

So extreme was the eclipse of Tenochca power that it can be said to have collapsed completely. The first hard blow struck by Cortés at the inception of the great siege of Mexico City caused the Tenochca warriors to flee, giving up the defense of their city into the hands of the Tlatilulca. The siege of Mexico is thus wrongly identified, for Mexico should be defined as an urban area housing both moieties of the Mexica, and this had ceased to exist at the fall of the Tenochca. The siege was more properly a fight for Tlatilulco alone. Civil war, preceding the Spanish attack, had dealt its deadly blow here as well. As in the case of Atauhuallpa, Cuauhtemoc represented only a part of his nation.

(6)

The fact that the Spanish entry came some time after the apogee of the two Amerindian states may have had something to do with the ease of the conquests. We cannot be certain, however. We can only assert that the conquests were greatly facilitated by the uncertainty and terror created among the people by the belief that the gods were returning.

Myths are never wholly accepted in any society. Some men resent certain myths and either criticize them or fail to find a place for them in their understanding. The myth of the return of the god and the consequent ending of the aeon did not command unanimous belief. Cuitlahuac and Cuauhtemoc, while in the entourage of Moteuczoma II, seem to have disagreed violently with the latter's opinion that the Spaniards were the expected gods. While Huascar and his party in Cuzco believed that the intruding Spaniards were indeed the expected gods, Atauhuallpa had no such illusions.

We can see, however, that for the period before the fateful landings and for a short time thereafter—long enough to sap what strength was left in the two imperial communities—the myth indeed was the key to their histories. Even geography helped to drive the nail home. Quetzalcoatl had disappeared into the east, coasting along the shores of the Gulf and promising to come back. Córdoba, Grijalva, and Cortés all came from exactly that same direction. Viracocha had disappeared into the Pacific off Ecuador in the north promising also to reappear, and it was in these same waters that Pizarro, on his second and third voyages, was to first reveal his presence. Sea voyages were indicated in both myths and the Spaniards in both instances had come by sea.

The first Spaniards in Mesoamerica were called "the gods" (*teules* in the careless Spanish writing of the day). Their counterparts in Peru were the *viracochas*. It is interesting that in both myths a plurality of beings had been indicated. Quetzalcoatl had left Tula with a whole entourage of followers. Viracocha was known to have had

angelic helpers around him, known collectively as viracochas and considered to be emanations of him. The
difference was that while Moteuczoma was reduced to
jelly by the invasion, certain that the invaders were gods,
Atauhuallpa doubted this and was prepared to confront
them as men. On the day just previous to his capture the
latter had in fact executed some of his court for the
cowardice which they had evinced when facing De Soto.

Yet both royal receptions, done from such divergent
assumptions, had exactly similar results: the capture of
the two emperors by miraculously easy Spanish stra-
tagems, each one adapted to the peculiar situation.

(7)

The fact that Moteuczoma and Atauhuallpa were both
seized by the Spaniards in the safety of their own courts
does not really enter our story. It has to do only with the
similarity in the plans and ambushes of the Spaniards,
and need not indulge our speculations.

Once arrested, however, and placed in captivity, the
tale falls again into our ambit and here we note differences. Though a captive, Atauhuallpa still exercised the
power of a sapay apu Inca even to the extent of ordering
the secret execution of Huascar, held captive by his
generals not too far to the south. With few exceptions his
followers remained loyal, and administratively, Tahuantinsuyo still held together. With Moteuczoma it was
different. Once captured he saw his support fall rapidly
away, the erosion being the inevitable result of his lack of
royal dignity, his treachery to his own party, and his
inconstancy. He could send out orders to a few parts of
his empire that were still obeyed but he could no longer

command the loyalty of his own people in Mexico. In their eyes he was unworthy of the office of tlatoani.

Surely these facts reflect a deep difference in the nature of the two states and their mission in history, the one an integrated empire, the other a conglomeration of conquests. At the end the sapay Inca was shored up by the fact of empire itself, an already achieved unity. Tahuantinsuyo gave to him who ruled it a more secular view of history, but at the same time tempted him to a mistaken sense of his own divinity. We see this in Atauhuallpa who displayed a fatal self-confidence, almost a feeling of omnipotence, which led directly to his capture. He publicly scorned the pitiful handful of Spaniards who had entered his realm and was unawed by popular opinion which thought them to be divine. Tahuantinsuyo had thus correctly led its rulers to penetrate the mists of superstition and myth upon which the very empire had been so painfully erected. Empire here had created a vantage point of detachment which could have led to astounding achievements. But this new secularity, this dispassion, peaked in one single office and could not in the short passage of the years indoctrinate the rank and file below. Tahuantinsuyo was a formula contained in one man's mind and was dependent on his courage and omnipresence. Atauhuallpa's courage was unquestioned; his inability to lend his spirit to the whole of the empire was what brought him down. And with his fall the majesty of Tahuantinsuyo incontinently passed away.

When a state such as Mexico appears in the midst of other similarly contentious states, it tends to grow without a myth of mission or, what is the same thing, without an orientation. No doubt this is the manner in which most communities are born. But this lack of an overmastering principle which is fervently believed in and served, means that the state will be prey to whatever powerful influences exist in the community. Mexico did not believe that it had been called into being on the world's first day. It was very conscious of the fact that it was the youngest city in the valley and one built upon slime. Thus the incumbent of the high office of tlatoani in Mexico could no more believe in the durability of the state than could its meanest citizen. The tlatoani was accordingly in no position to resist the ancient oracles which demanded not that the state be considered holy but that war be considered divine. Moteuczoma's final cowardice came from his religious sensibilities and from the almost priestly character of his office. He did not believe that the many conquests of Mexico had created something new in the world. These conquests were only accumulated booty and had been incidental to constant and bloody warfare. The ruler's view was that of any teuctli, intensified perhaps by being pinnacled and isolated in the seat of rule, but not essentially different. Accordingly, in the crisis he immunized himself from the events of his day and thus appears to us lacking in stature and manly dignity. Had Moteuczoma had an imperial theory of substance behind him he might well have acted differently.

After the fall of Mexico in 1521 and after the end of the Incas' attempt to retake Cuzco in 1537, both empires disappeared *de facto* (though continued on a much reduced scale *de jure*). The Spaniards in the critical but brief period between conquest and the establishment of their own state needed the pretense and the convenience of continued Indian rule. Thus, for a brief period Cuauhtemoc and Manco Inca ostensibly ruled each in his office. The sequel to this is fascinating.

Cuauhtemoc, along with the puppet rulers of Tezcoco and Tlacopan, was hanged by Cortés in 1525 without as much as a ripple disturbing the inertness of the conquered Aztecs. How different it was with the Incas! Manco Inca in 1536 summoned up the mighty ghost of Tahuantinsuyo and called upon it to reject the Spanish lords and regain the sacred city of Cuzco. In the next year and only after sustained fighting that effort collapsed, and in 1538 Manco Inca was forced to retire over the Andes with a rump nation to carry on as best he could. This pathetic but persistent neo-Inca state lasted under four increasingly weak emperors until 1572 when the last of them was captured and beheaded in Cuzco. Only then did Tahuantinsuyo as a memory die.

Herein we can see down into the basement of the political achievements of our two peoples, into their strengths and weaknesses.

My statements up to now may seem to have given all the kudos to the Incas, correspondingly demeaning the Mexica for not having built a more lasting political state and a more sufficient empire. It may seem to the reader that I have castigated the Mexica for their awful and uncontrolled thirst for blood while playing down the terrorism of the Incas.

On the level—that of every man's need to judge what was good and what was bad in the past—this is certainly true. But there are more profound levels of appreciation and from these levels the matter looks vastly different.

Speakers of Nahuatl, among whom were the Mexica, had a rhetorical mode of address we might at first glance consider curious. Certainly it appears overly artificial. It consisted of the avoidance of flat statements and the casting of one's thought into a recurrent mood of dubiety and questioning. The Mexica when discussing mankind's destiny preferred not to speak or think in dogmatic utterances. He professed doubt and ignorance:

And behold, verily now, what doth our lord desire?
Perhaps we shall obtain something as merit? Something as dessert? Perhaps we shall merit that of which
we here dream, that which we here see in dreams.
We speak in the land of the dead.

The Mexica never factored out of their cultural experience any concrete image of certainty, as the Incas did with
Tahuantinsuyo, because they could not believe that anything on earth could be that certain. They experienced life
as dream configurations and reversals. They were too
deeply pessimistic to believe that the state, crazy instrument that it was, could ever be an enduring *civitas terrena.*
They doubted its eternity and their myths therefore
neglected it. They were a people not unhappy so much as
unaware of joy. Their lives were endowed with fears and
paralyzing terrors, but they endured as they might and
lived out their lives in service. That they sought to pay
their great debt in hearts and blood is revolting and
unfortunate, but that they insisted on paying it at all to
their proper masters, the gods, was right and correct. One
indeed might indict the Incas for hiding from themselves
the truth of their debt to the heavens and pretending that
they were the gods and that all men owed all things to
them.

After all, Tahuantinsuyo can with plausibility be
looked upon as a fortress within which a people took
refuge lest they should learn to think. It is moot as to
whether a national institution or the quality of a communal life is of greater import in history.

EPILOGUE

When the man of the Aztec world gazed up to the thirteen heavens into which the firmament was divided, he was contemplating a priestly construction, probably very old and certainly not his own. From its teaching he knew himself to be a lonely fighter in a lost cause and his deepest appreciation of the universe conformed to that stern thought.

Two things to him were real. One was the earth which he walked upon and which he likened to a cosmic crocodilian monster—the peaked mountains were the scales upon its back and its jaws gaped constantly to swallow him up. Death was everywhere, a chilling specter clearly allied to the earth and inhabiting its deepest parts. The five directions—east, north, west, south and center —were aspects of this inescapable tellurian presence. As one turned on his heel, one moved through gigantic cycles of meaning all stored up in the earth and symbolized directionally.

The other reality was the world of time and the astral bodies. As contrasted with the earth which was heavy, inert, and inexorable, this other was a kinetic world where forces of opposites were in perilous turmoil, where there was the constant drama of confrontation: of the jubilant morning sun as against his hopeless, embered self of the evening; of the azure of day and the funereal obscurity of night; of days of evil omen as against days of strength and success. Out of this second world the Aztec made a cultural home for himself. He imagined this world as warfare. Herein at least he could behold the splendor and the heroism of physical combat as when the sun and the morning star attempted to slay each other. Yet battle-grounds also end in death so he came to the same conclusion in considering this second world as he had in gazing down at the first. The difference was that this one invited his activity—even if only momentarily.

These two cosmic stereotypes were never mated in the Aztec's understanding. They existed side by side and were both accepted but they did not interpenetrate. It is this fact more than anything else which rendered the man from Mexico so violent and in a sense so pathetic.

The Inca also knew both the heavens and the earth as abodes of different supernatural meaning, but he was not disturbed. In his somewhat stuffy arrogance and childlike simplicity he imposed on the cosmos the imperial con-cept—where there is empire there is an emperor. He crowned Viracocha with sovereignty and imagined that all the other lesser supernaturals somehow or other ac-quiesced in this dominion. Neither earth nor sun and stars appeared to challenge this. However various the attributes of the many gods and huacas, the cosmos was indeed one. This freed the Inca for the administrative tasks of his day. It was not that he was less religious than the Aztec; he was simply more confident, less aware of the mutability of human affairs, freer to build historic tools and institutions and to assign to them pragmatic values. It would be wrong to say that the Inca was an optimist while the Aztec was a pessimist. The former was simply less bedeviled with thoughts and regrets.

At great cost to themselves men in history create structures of society. These, in turn, dictate their response to sudden events or changed circumstances. Why the

Mexica and Inca should have differed so is a mystery for which we shall never have an answer but which we must acknowledge to be proof of the freedom of man's spirit. In spite of amazing similarities in background, social status, early struggles, and crucial victories at like moments, these two peoples fabricated contrasting or, at the most, complementary views of the cosmos. On the minority status of man as opposed to the primacy of the divine they agreed. Beyond that and in all details they differed. This is a very strange matter. It is a fundamental paradox.

BIBLIOGRAPHY

This bibliography is intended only to introduce the reader in a preliminary fashion to some of the more generally available works in English on the Aztecs and Incas.

Anderson, A. J. O. and Dibble, Charles E. (translators). *Florentine Codex: General History of the Things of New Spain* (by Fray Bernardino de Sahagún). 12 vols. Santa Fe: School of American Research, 1950–70. These volumes form the single most valuable native source on the history and culture of the Aztecs. The Nahuatl and English translations are set side by side. There is a revised edition of volume one.

Brundage, Burr C. *Empire of the Inca.* Norman, Oklahoma: University of Oklahoma Press, 1973. A complete history of the Inca people and the political structures they built from the beginnings to 1533. Based exclusively on source materials.

———. *Lords of Cuzco.* Norman, Oklahoma: University of Oklahoma Press, 1967. A detailed account of the events under Huascar, last legitimate Inca emperor, and carrying the story down to the execution of Tupac Amaru in 1572. The intent of this volume, however, is mainly to display the social and ceremonial life of the Inca people. It thus complements the former volume. Based on source materials only.

———. *A Rain of Darts: The History of the Mexica Aztecs.* Austin, Texas: University of Texas Press, 1972. A full history, concentrating on the political and military events of that Aztec people known as the Mexica. The story ends with the fall of Tenochtitlan/Tlatilulco in 1521. The original sources have been thoroughly utilized.

Caso, Alfonso. *People of the Sun.* Norman, Oklahoma: University of Oklahoma Press, 1958. A dependable interpretation of the Aztecs by one of the most distinguished workers in the field.

The Handbook of Middle American Indians, 15 vols. University of Texas Press, Austin, 1964–75. One of the great reference works prepared by outstanding scholars. Scattered throughout the fifteen volumes are materials on the Aztecs.

Katz, Friedrich. *The Great American Civilizations.* London: Weidenfeld and Nicholson, 1972. A recent and comprehensive view of both Inca and Aztec culture in one volume with supporting material on their historical and archaeological backgrounds. Useful bibliography.

Keen, Benjamin (ed. and translator). *Life and Labor in Ancient Mexico* (a translation of the *Brief and Summary Relation* written by Alonso de Zorita). New Brunswick, New Jersey: Rutgers University Press, 1963. Zorita was a humane and observant public servant in early colonial times. His work is one of the important sources on Aztec landholding, tribute, social structure, etc. Keen's introduction is also enlightening.

Kubler, George. *The Art and Architecture of Ancient America.* Harmondsworth, England: Penguin Books, 1962. A professional survey of the aesthetic components of the cultures of Nuclear America. As such it includes cultures such as the Maya, Chavín, Muisca, etc., as well as Inca and Aztec. It is useful therefore for placing the two latter cultures in comparisons with the other Indian cultures.

León-Portilla, Miguel (ed.). *The Broken Spears, the Aztec Account of the Conquest of Mexico.* Boston: Beacon Press, 1962. A translation of selected passages out of the original Nahuatl. This is highly recommended to all readers as an antidote to a constant diet of Spanish accounts which present only the views of the conquerors. It is rare that posterity acquires such an intimate and moving account of a great military confrontation from the lips of the conquered.

———. *Aztec Thought and Culture, A Study of the Ancient Nahuatl Mind.* Norman, Oklahoma: University of Oklahoma Press, 1963. This is the standard work on the subject of Aztec ideas about god, man, and the universe. In all cases León-Portilla bases his assertions on the texts themselves, of which he is one of the foremost translators.

———. *Pre-Columbian Literatures of Mexico.* Norman, Oklahoma: University of Oklahoma Press, 1969. A short but useful survey of the prose, poetry, and chronicles of the Mesoamerican peoples, mainly Aztecs. Lengthy selections of the translated texts are interspersed with the commentary.

Livermore, Harold V. (ed. and translator). *Royal Commentaries of the Incas and General History of Peru* (by Garcilaso de la Vega). 2 vols. Austin, Texas: University of Texas Press, 1966. A fine and complete translation of the most famous primary work on the Incas. Garcilaso is a fascinating person and this book is an item in world literature. It must be used, however, with caution, particularly in the parts devoted to history and chronology.

Mason, J. Alden. *The Ancient Civilizations of Peru.* Rev. ed. Harmondsworth, England: Penguin Books, 1968. An excellent and scholarly survey of all of the prehistoric cultures of Peru with at least a third of the work devoted to the Incas.

Moore, Sally F. *Power and Property in Inca Peru.* New York: Columbia University Press, 1958. This work discusses such items as law, tribute, forms of land tenure, etc. among the Inca.

De Onis, Harriet (translator). *The Incas of Cieza de León.* Norman, Oklahoma: University of Oklahoma Press, 1959. Good, clear translations of selections of the important work of Cieza de León, one of the early and more likable of the Spanish conquistadors. The selections have been arranged by the editor

Victor von Hagen whose main interest has been in the Inca road system. There are copious explanatory footnotes.

Rowe, John H. "Inca Culture at the Time of the Spanish Conquest." *Handbook of the South American Indians,* vol. 2. Julian H. Steward, ed. Washington, D.C.: Smithsonian Institution, 1945–48. This thorough work is the equivalent in Inca studies of the works of Soustelle and Vaillant in the Aztec field. A vast amount of cultural information is here packed into the small space of about 150 pages. Rowe is one of the leading Peruvianists.

Soustelle, Jacques. *The Daily Life of the Aztecs.* Harmondsworth, England: Penguin Books, 1964. This is perhaps the best survey of the thought, religion, and culture of the Aztecs.

Vaillant, George C. *Aztecs of Mexico.* Rev. ed., Harmondsworth, England: Penguin Books, 1966. About two-thirds of this book is devoted to the Aztec civilization, the rest being given over to predecessor cultures. It has some excellent tables concerned with rituals, deities, and the calendar.

INDEX